Greek Islands
of the Aegean

Greek Islands

Text by Lindsay Bennett
Editor: Erica Spaberg Keirstead
Photography: Pete Bennett
Cover photograph by Pete Bennett
Layout: Media Content Marketing, Inc.
Cartography by Raffaele Degennaro
Managing Editor: Tony Halliday

Fifth Edition 2002

CONTACTING THE EDITORS
Every effort has been made to provide accurate information in this publication, but
changes are inevitable. The publisher cannot be responsible for any resulting loss,
inconvenience or injury. We would appreciate it if readers would call our attention to
any errors or outdated information by contacting Berlitz Publishing, PO Box 7910,
London SE1 1WE, England. Fax: (44) 20 7403 0290;
e-mail: berlitz@apaguide.demon.co.uk

CONTENTS

The Greek Islands and Their People   7

A Brief History   13

Where to Go   25

The Cyclades   28
The Dodecanese   51
The Eastern Aegean   61
The Northern Aegean   70
The Sporades   74

What to Do	79
Sports	80
Shopping	84
Entertainment	87
Activities for Children	90
Eating Out	93
Handy Travel Tips	102
Hotels and Restaurants	128
Index	142

● A ☞ in the text denotes a highly recommended sight

Greek Islands
of the Aegean

THE GREEK ISLANDS AND THEIR PEOPLE

The classical gods made their home here, fighting their battles, having their love affairs, and giving birth to their children. The Persians coveted them over 7,000 years ago, and they were stepping-stones on the long East–West trading routes throughout Hellenistic and Roman times. Throughout most of the last two millennia, they were fought over by European superpowers and became pawns in the religious conflicts between Christianity and Islam. Although they now form part of the modern state of Greece, a deep imprint of history's footsteps can be seen clearly on every dusty hill, in every olive grove, and along every coastline. Today, with their hot summer days, warm waters, abundant beaches, and distinct lifestyle, the Greek islands of the Aegean are among the major tourist playgrounds in the world.

The Aegean is a small sea, a finger of water 640 km (397 miles) long, and 320 km (198 miles) wide, pointing up out of the eastern Mediterranean between the modern states of Greece and Turkey. Its more than 1,400 islands, although scattered, form a series of groups, each with its own particular character. This guide will introduce you to many, but not all, of the popular Aegean Islands.

The most accessible islands from Athens are the Cyclades to the southeast, thrown like a handful of pebbles into the sea. In ancient times, they sat in a circle (*cyclos*) around the sacred island of Delos, and their name has carried through into modern times. The islands' barren landscapes and stark white, cubical houses with their blue-shuttered windows bedecked with geraniums represent the Greek islands to many. The most popular and best known are the lively island of Mykonos and the awe-inspiring caldera of Santorini.

Collected together in the southeastern reaches of the Aegean Sea are the Dodecanese islands. They rest against the southwest corner of the Turkish coastline. The major island in the group is Rhodes (covered in its own *Berlitz Pocket Guide*), but others include Kos and Patmos. In the eastern Aegean, three of its larger islands mirror the western Turkish coastline. Lesvos, Chios, and Samos still have many vestiges of the traditional rural lifestyle that made them rich and coveted during previous centuries.

In the northern Aegean are three more disparate islands — Thasos, Limnos, and Samothraki — while southwest of these, closer to Athens, are the Sporades islands of Skiathos, Skopelos, Alonissos, and Skyros — until recently the exclusive playground of the Greek jet set.

The volatile and fascinating history of the whole area means that no two islands are identical, although similarities do exist. Despite countless different landlords, the basic ele-

What's in a Name?

There are no hard and fast rules that govern the roman transliterations of Greek place names on maps and road signs. Indeed, you will often find the same village name spelled differently on two consecutive road signs. Some names, such as *Chios* and *Hios*, are easily recognized as interchangeable, but others can be confusing.

This guide uses the spellings that are generally accepted in Western Europe, but you will find variations, since the Greek alphabet does not directly match the Roman alphabet.

The islands also can shun Western names. Santorini is Italian for Saint Irene, the name given to the island in Byzantine times when the saint is believed to have died there. The island's ancient (and official) name is Thira, which is used by airlines and ferry companies on their tickets and printed schedules.

ments of the way of life of ordinary people have changed little for over 5,000 years. The seas produced abundant food for the earliest settlers, and the warm summers brought forth crops of grain that sustained humans and provided grazing for herds of goats from the fifth century B.C. onward.

Since the Bronze Age, donkeys and mules have provided a means of transport; around the same time, the first olives and vines were planted in the ground. Life was governed by seasons of planting, tending,

Still going strong — donkeys have been used for transport since the Bronze Age.

and harvesting. Look around the Greek islands today and there is little cause to think that much has changed.

Tradition plays a great part in island lifestyle. The sexes still lead separate lives, with the women in the home, chatting across balconies festooned with washing or sitting on shady street corners. The men work in the fields or at their boats, with older men at the *kafeneion* or coffee shop — where the world is put to rights over a strong *café ellenikos.*

The family is the core of daily life. Children, especially boys, are seen as a blessing and are treated with indulgence, fussed over by mothers and grandmothers. Grandparents and fathers push the carriages of the new arrivals during the evening *volta,* or stroll, glowing in the warmth of the congratulations of their neighbors and friends. Fathers and uncles employ sons and nephews in family businesses, before any outsider.

The siesta is an important part of the day. Everyone from the youngest to the oldest rests during the heat of the afternoon and makes the most of the cool evenings, often not going to bed until well after midnight.

Historically, the fabric of life has been sustained by religion. Indeed, the church, and the Orthodox religion, was identified with all that was Greek long before the modern state was created in 1832. Through natural disaster, war, and disease, the church has been there as a place of refuge and solace, both physically and spiritually. To this day, the priest has a strong influence within the community. Women have traditionally formed the majority of the congregation, praying for the protection of their fathers, husbands, and sons while they were

Though the fishing industry has largely been eclipsed by tourism, some still make their living the traditional way.

away at sea in merchant fleets, diving for sponges, or working in lands far away. The smallest whitewashed churches house a simple cross, icon, and lit candles, although you will find the largest churches are somewhat more lavish and ornate.

Greece once had the largest merchant fleet in the world, and the sea still plays a major role in the life of the Aegean. On smaller, more remote islands, ferries form the only transportation link with the outside world. They carry essential goods, just as they have done throughout history. Each island has a flotilla of small craft setting sail daily to bring fresh catch to the island's tables.

However, tourism has begun to alter this long-standing scenario. It is now the biggest money earner in the islands. In high season, you will share your Greek odyssey with visitors from almost every country in Europe, and increasingly from around the world. This has saved many islands from the brink of poverty and depopulation, although it is undoubtedly affecting the character of many of the more popular islands. Island society has seen more change in the last twenty years than in the previous thousand.

Today, motor scooters often drown the sound of playing children, and mobile phones are heard far more frequently than the haunting cadences of the *bazouki*. More often than not, the harried man walking briskly along the street while taking his call — often waving an arm in animated fashion — has a busi-

Aromatic Air

The scent of herbs on the hillsides — or grown in pots in doorways — is one of the most distinctive aspects of Greek life. Basil *(basilicum)* has long been a friend of Greek kitchens. Its scent is said to keep insects at bay. Brush your hand against the leaves and smell the fragrance: it will instantly refresh you on a hot day.

ness empire of restaurants, car-rental agencies, ticket offices, and studio apartments to manage. He needs to keep his finger on the pulse to succeed during the short tourist season.

As incomes rise, the young farmer buys a truck to replace his father's trusty donkey, or he gives up farming altogether to open a bar or car-rental office. The fisherman uses his boat to ferry tourists to nearby beaches rather than to catch fish.

But the picture is not quite as bleak as it is painted. Tourism too is a seasonal industry, fitting neatly into the traditional cyclical pattern of island life. In spring, before the tourists arrive, goats and sheep give birth and their herds head out to the open pasture; a little later, the grain crop is harvested. As autumn approaches, another harvest begins. Olives, walnuts, almonds, and late developing fruit must all be brought in and preserved before the start of winter.

So in a sense, island life continues just as it always has!

What's in a name? Plenty, it seems, for these ardent fans of Mykonos's Paradise Beach — one of many island idylls.

A BRIEF HISTORY

Prehistoric man in Asia Minor (now modern Turkey) or Greece could look out across the Aegean toward the horizon and see the faint silhouette of land. Their curiosity pushed them to build vessels that were strong enough to ford the open seas and reach these islands, marking the start of the long legacy of Mediterranean seafaring.

Around 7000 B.C., the Phoenicians set out from what is now Iran to explore their surroundings. They eventually reached the islands, and founded colonies on the islands in the northernmost part of the Aegean Sea. An important early material, obsidian, was discovered on the island of Milos. Obsidian is a hard, vitreous volcanic rock, which could be fashioned into tools for cutting and stabbing. The high quality of the seam on Milos ensured that the area remained popular with early travelers.

The basic elements of life in the Aegean began to come together as early as 5000 B.C., and were already in place by the late Bronze Age (c. 2700 B.C.). The major changes were not to daily tasks and routines, but to the political power base, which changed regularly and not necessarily peacefully throughout the ages.

Cycladic Culture

At around 3500 B.C., a sophisticated culture evolved in the Cyclades islands. The distinctive, sculpted marble figures of the era are now being reproduced in vast quantities as souvenirs. You will find original examples in the archaeological museums throughout the Cyclades, although one of the earliest examples is in the museum on Paros. The people farmed and fished; on the dawning of the Bronze Age in 2700 B.C., they began to work with metals. The Cycladic culture was influ-

Notes from the past — Classical Greek stone carvings in Kos Town's agora.

enced by societies in the east, importing the pottery wheel from Mesopotamia. They also continued to trade in obsidian and the local marble.

The Minoans and the Myceneans

Farther south in Crete, the Minoan culture developed after 2000 B.C. into the most significant of its age, spreading its influence throughout the region by trade and diplomacy. Santorini (Thira), the next major island north, was heavily influenced by Crete, and the settlements of Thira and Akrotiri thrived at this time. The magnificent frescoes and mosaics found at Akrotiri are in Athens at present, but the remains of the buildings at the site provide ample evidence of the sophistication of the culture here.

Around 1500 B.C., a massive volcanic eruption at Santorini destroyed not only Akrotiri — under feet of ash and pumice — but the whole Minoan civilization. Massive tidal waves swept over Crete, and other parts of the Mediterranean, smashing buildings and drowning many thousands of people.

In the wake of this tremendous natural upheaval, the Aegean Islands next came under the influence of the Myceneans (at around 1300 B.C.), who had a base in the Peloponnese region of the Greek mainland. The Myceneans were an acquisitive race who came to conquer, not to trade. Their extensive military campaigns were later chronicled by Homer in his epic poems *The Odyssey* and *The Iliad.*

The Rise of Athens

The Dorians, who came overland from northern Europe, conquered the Mycenaeans. They were a barbaric race, and their custody of the area brought about a dark period during which the written word was forgotten and art disappeared. They held sway over islands off the northern Greek coast, but the Phoenicians kept control of the main sea routes; south of the area, trade continued as usual. At the same time, city-states began to grow in influence on the southern Greek mainland. Athens became the most powerful, heralding the start of the classical Greek period. However, Greece was not yet a country; each city-state was self-governing and autonomous.

The new culture spread throughout the Mediterranean, helped by a huge increase in migration from the mainland to new settlements such as Carthage, a Greek city on the African coast of the Mediterranean. Culture and the arts flourished once again. Athletic prowess was admired and the Olympic games were constituted in 776 B.C., to promote friendly competition. Homer wrote his epic works on Chios; and lyrical poetry was much admired, particularly the work of the poets Archilochos on Paros and Sappho on Lesvos.

The preeminent islands of this era were Delos, a sacred island and center of religion ruled by Athens; Samos, ruled by the tyrant Polycrates; and Naxos, whose ruler Lygdamis undertook some major building projects. Archaeology shows that, during this time, societies lived mainly in coastal trading towns with little settlement inland.

The Persian Wars

As Athens rose in influence and power in the West, it was matched in the East by the rise of the Persian Empire. From a power base in Anatolia, the Persians overran the eastern Aegean Islands and set their sights on the Cyclades. In 490 B.C., they captured sacred Delos and razed the settlements on Naxos. The island communities were undecided about which side to back for a time. Paros and Andros contributed to the Persian armory, while others supported Athens. The two superpowers finally clashed at the epic battles of Marathon and Salamis in 480 B.C. The Persians were defeated, and Athens duly punished the islands that had turned against it.

Following its victory, Athens introduced the concept of a mutual protection alliance (a kind of NATO of the ancient

Archaeological treasures such as these stone reliefs abound in Delos, and recall Greece's formidable ancient past.

world). Several islands and Greek city-states agreed to work together, and created a treasury to fund their plans, which was held on the island of Delos. The alliance became known as the Delian League. Although there were minor internal wrangles, the league controlled the Aegean and the greater Athenian Empire for most of the fifth century B.C. Later, in 454 B.C., the treasury was transferred to Athens and its deposits were used to finance the construction of many of the major buildings and temples of the Classical Age.

In 431 B.C., Athens began a war with its neighbor and league member Sparta. Although the islands saw little action, as the war went on they could see that Athens was slowly losing its power. Before the end of the war in 401 B.C., many islands had already transferred their allegiance to the victors, who were led by Philip II of Macedon. He was followed in 336 B.C. by his son Alexander the Great, one of the most remarkable leaders in history. His rise to power ushered in the Hellenistic period.

Hellenistic and Roman Periods

When Alexander went on to conquer lands as far to the east as India, the Aegean became a crossroads for the long trading routes. Delos became one of the largest marketplaces in the empire. Following Alexander's death, his lands were divided among his generals. Much of the Aegean came under the rule of the Ptolemies, along with Egypt. Cleopatra was a member of this famous ruling clan.

Although in 88 B.C., Mithradates made a swift and successful raid from the East across Asia Minor and the Aegean Islands, the next major power change brought influence from the West. The Greek Hellenistic Empire was gradually, and peacefully, absorbed into the Roman Empire.

The Byzantine Empire and the Coming of Christianity

The Romans ruled a pagan empire, but the Aegean had an important influence on the early development of Christianity. In A.D. 95, St. John arrived on Patmos, a small rocky island in the Dodecanese, as a political prisoner. It was here that he wrote what was to become the final book of the New Testament, the Book of Revelation. It wasn't until A.D. 330, however, when the newly converted Emperor Constantine made Byzantium, renamed Constantinople, capital of his Eastern Empire that Christianity was assured of its dominant role in future Greek life.

The Byzantine Empire had powerful and well-fortified cities, but the countryside and the outlying islands were ravaged by waves of invaders. In an attempt to counter a threat from the Saracen Muslims, a new potent religious force from the East, the Byzantine army forcefully enlisted the men of the islands. Disease took a further toll. By the time of the Crusades, many of the Aegean islands had been practically depopulated.

As the Byzantine Empire weakened at the end of the first millennium, Crusader forces were sent from Western Europe to counter the Muslim forces and retake Jerusalem for the Christian faith. Unfortunately, their zeal was not matched by their discrimination. The crusaders swept through the l;and of Byzantium slaughtering Christians as well as Muslims, civilians as well as soldiers. Constantinople was taken by Crusader forces in 1204, and they stripped the city of many of its finest treasures — which now grace the public buildings of Venice — although a large consignment of books and manuscripts was transferred to the monastery at Patmos before the city fell.

While Byzantine land was being divided, there was no one in control of the seas, so pirates raided towns on many of the islands. To counter this, the populations moved from their homes on the coast and built settlements inland, out of sight of the raiding parties. This created a pattern seen today throughout the Aegean of a small port (*skala*) which serves an inland settlement or *chora*, making it easier to protect the island from attack.

The minor Aegean Islands were taken by various powerful European noblemen, many of whom were Genoese or Venetian, such as Marco Sanudo on Naxos. The noblemen had free rein to create their own fiefdoms. The

Traditional egg tempera icons reflect Greek Orthodoxy in all its Byzantine splendor.

Venetians fortified their main towns — Naxos Town and Antiparos Town are wonderful examples of this — creating labyrinths of narrow alleys and cul-de-sacs that were designed to confuse and to demoralize invaders. The Genoese took control of the eastern Aegean Islands, which were considered the most valuable for agriculture and trade.

After a final bloody defeat by the Muslims in 1309, Christian forces were forced from the Holy Land. The Knights of St. John, a holy military force, made their way to Rhodes and Kos in the Dodecanese. They began the process of building their strong citadels, and reinforcing the Christian faith on the islands. However, they had not seen the last of their Muslim foe. A force was gaining strength in the east to threaten their new bases.

The Coming of the Ottoman Turks

The Ottomans were roving invaders who came from the east, taking land in what is now Turkey. By the end of the 13th century, they began their first raids on the Aegean Islands. In 1453, they took Constantinople, and immediately made it their capital, renaming it Istanbul.

They then set their sights on the islands of the Knights of St. John and, after an unsuccessful siege in 1480, they finally ejected the knights from the Dodecanese in 1522. In 1566, they wrested Chios from the Genoese, bolstering their hold on the eastern Aegean Islands, but the Cyclades remained in Venetian hands for another generation or more — Tinos was the last to fall in 1715. The Ottomans brought new influences to the islands that they controlled, forming a large empire that stretched around the eastern Mediterranean.

Toward Greek Independence

However, a movement was growing on the Greek peninsula against Ottoman rule and for an independent Greek state. In 1770, Russia came to aid the Greeks (defined by their Orthodox religion rather than by historical geographical boundaries), declaring war on the Ottoman Empire and occupying several Aegean islands until 1774. Graffiti written by Russian soldiers can be seen in the caves of Antiparos.

Although this attempt was unsuccessful, the campaign for a Greek state continued into the 19th century and began to grow in strength. The Aegean Islands played their part. Lesvos, Chios, and Samos lay in the important shipping lanes, and patriots began disrupting Ottoman cargo traffic. In return, the Turks violently put down every insurrection, including the massacre on Chios, when 22,000 people were slaughtered.

The Ottoman Empire was weakening, however, and in 1821, the peoples of the Greek mainland achieved nationhood for the first time. The Cyclades and the Sporades island chains were also included in this new state. A new sense of identity enveloped Greek peoples throughout the Aegean, thus commencing a movement to expand Greece and unify the disparate Orthodox populations.

The Twentieth Century

A series of disastrous decisions at the beginning of the 20th century began to sound a death knell for the Ottoman Empire. The Turks lost a short war with Italy, and were forced to relinquish the Dodecanese islands to the Italians. Greece took this opportunity to absorb the islands of the northern and eastern Aegean and to add Macedonia to its mainland territories.

Following this debacle, the Ottomans then allied themselves to Germany in the World War I, losing more territory with the defeat of the Germans in that war. Greece was handed a strip of land along the western coast of Asia Minor, which for over 2,000 years had had a substantial Greek population. Greece moved in to administer the land, but a new influence upset any grand dreams of making this region a part of greater Greece.

In 1923, Turkey broke away from the tired Ottoman rulers, and Kemal Ataturk rose to power on a wave of popular support. He promised a modern state for his people, but as the situation became volatile, civil strife broke out in Turkish cities, and those considered Greek were victims of threats and violence. Many had to leave their birthplaces, fleeing to Lesvos, Chios, and Samos, the Greek-ruled islands just offshore. Thousands of people arrived with little more than the clothes they wore, putting great strain on the resources of the islands. Finally, Greece was ousted from its new territory in Asia Minor, which became part of the new Turkish state.

Greece attempted to stay out of World War II, but Mussolini saw Greece as an ideal addition to his Italian empire. His forces made a series of attacks from their bases in the Dodecanese islands, including sinking a Greek naval vessel in the harbor of Tinos Town, but they only succeeded in strengthening the resolve of the population against them. Later the Germans came in force and occupied many of the islands.

After the war, in 1949, the Dodecanese islands finally became part of the Greek nation. But the country was politically fragmented, with arguments between monarchists and republicans, right and left, and tension escalated into civil war. The struggle bypassed most of the islands, although there was fierce fighting on Samos. Even after the fighting stopped more than a decade later, the country was not stable.

At the same time, the massive growth in air and road transport saw shipping decline in importance. The Aegean

See me, touch me, heal me! The Hippocrates monument in Kos stands in honor of the father of modern medicine.

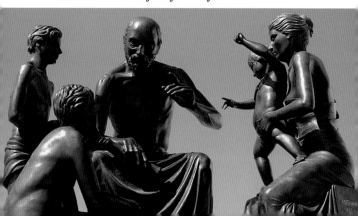

Islands, which for centuries had been important ports on the trading routes, became the backwaters of this new transport network and the economies of several islands came close to collapse.

In 1967, the military took the reins of power in Athens, and until 1974, the "Colonels" held sway with a repressive and brutal regime. Many Greek islanders chose to leave rather than live in poverty and terror, and many made new homes in the United States and Australia. The expansion of air travel began the age of mass tourism, and Greece along with the Aegean Islands became exciting destinations for northern Europeans escaping their damp, cool summers.

In 1982, Greece joined the European Common Market (now the European Union). Since this time, membership has been of great monetary benefit to the country. The EU has given large subsidies to develop Greece's infrastructure and grants to excavate and protect its ancient monuments.

Airfields have been constructed on a number of the islands, and road systems have been expanded and improved. Private investment has even made an increasingly modern ferry fleet possible.

Politically, the end of the 20th century was a relatively quiet time for the islands, although the divorce of Greek prime minister Andreas Papandreou (died 1996) and his subsequent marriage to a much younger woman caused consternation within conservative Greek society.

As the Balkans flared to war once again, Greek nationalism stirred, and there have been discussions in the *kafeneion* about the land of Macedonia returning to the fold of its forefathers. Whether this will ever happen remains to be seen, but perhaps the aid offered by Greece to Turkey after 1999's devastating earthquake is a sign that the animosity between these two traditional enemies is beginning to diminish.

Historical Landmarks

7000 B.C. Phoenicians explore the Aegean.

3000 B.C. Bronze Age culture thrives in the Cyclades.

2000 B.C. Minoan culture dominates the Aegean.

1500 B.C. The volcano on Santorini erupts, destroying Minoan civilization.

1450 B.C. The Mycenaean culture becomes dominant.

1100-750 B.C. Dorian invasion brings a dark period to the Aegean.

500 B.C. Persian forces overrun many Aegean islands, until they are defeated by the Athenians in 480 B.C.

477 B.C. Athens founds the Delian League.

366 B.C. Alexander the Great rules Greece and the islands.

31 B.C. The Romans annex all Greek territory.

A.D. 95–323 St. John writes The Book of Revelation on Patmos. Constantine founds the Byzantine Empire; two churches develop, the Orthodox in Constantinople, and the Catholic in Rome.

800-1000 Muslim forces attack the islands.

tenth-12th centuries Holy Crusades lead to the breakdown of the Byzantine Empire.

1309 The Knights of St. John take the Dodecanese islands.

1450-1566 The Ottomans take first Constantinople (renaming it Istanbul), then the Dodecanese islands, and finally, Chios.

1821 Greek War of Independence. Ottomans crush the opposition.

1832 The Cyclades and Sporades island chains are included in the new Greek state.

1912-1913 The Balkans War sees Greece taking the northern and eastern Aegean Islands from Turkey. The Dodecanese islands are ceded in trust to Italy.

1939-1944 Greece sides with the Allies after being attacked by Italian forces.

1944-1949 Civil war in Greece largely bypasses the islands.

1949 The Dodecanese islands become part of Greece.

1967-1974 Military dictatorship; massive emigration results.

1982 Greece joins the European Union (EU).

WHERE TO GO

Finding the most suitable Greek island for your style of vacation is important, as each group of islands, as well as each individual island, is unique. Do you want sun-kissed beaches, nonstop nightlife, ancient sites to explore, or traditional Greek family life around you?

Most islands will have a little of each of these elements, but some, such as Ios, have given themselves over to party tourism almost completely. In summer, there is little traditional activity for you to enjoy. Equally, islands such as Lesvos or Chios have few nightclubs. Here you'll find much more evidence of the rural life, with olive groves and livestock farms in the hilly interiors.

In this edition, we have divided the Aegean Islands into five groups. The odyssey starts with the Cyclades islands, the most accessible island chain from Athens, the capital of Greece. Next, traveling counterclockwise, we reach the Dodecanese islands in the southeastern Aegean (excluding Rhodes, which is covered in its own *Berlitz Pocket Guide*). We then move on to the eastern Aegean islands of Samos, Chios, and Lesvos, which sit parallel to the Turkish mainland, and the northern Aegean islands of Samothraki, Limnos, and Thasos. We conclude with the Sporades islands.

We have concentrated on the major islands in each group. However, you'll also find concise information about some of the smaller or more remote islands within the larger island groups, such as the Cyclades and the Dodecanese, to help you plan any island-hopping you might want to undertake.

Getting Around

Connections among the island chains are poor, with the exception of the ports of Piraeus and Rafina on the Greek mainland, which serve as transportation hubs for those who wish to travel from one chain of islands to another. However, within each chain (particularly the Cyclades, the Dodecanese, and the Sporades), ferry connections are regular and journey times are relatively short. Car ferries are the slowest of the transportation options, but their stately progress allows you to enjoy the sun and sea air from their promenade and sun decks. Both hydrofoils and large, powerful catamarans will cut ferry journey times in half; however you will sit in an air-conditioned interior cabin for the duration of your ride.

Once on a particular island, you can easily get around on foot or rent a car for more in-depth exploring. Also, most towns on smaller islands are linked by a good bus system.

Within the Cyclades, Dodecanese, and Sporades island groups, there are certain towns that serve as hubs for travel

Day-tripping in style! A caique unloads eager island-hoppers in Mykonos.

to and from other islands within each group. Below is a list of the hubs and the islands that can be reached by ferry from them within two hours. From Mykonos, you can travel to Delos, Paros, Naxos, Tinos, Andros, and Syros. From Skiathos, you can reach Skopelos, Allonissos, and Skyros. From Kos, you can reach Patmos, Kalymnos, Nyssiros, and the medieval citadel at Rhodes (covered in the *Berlitz Pocket Guide to Rhodes*).

The overseas offices of the Greek National Tourist Organization (GNTO) carry current schedules for the major ferry services. The web site (www.gtpnet.com) also lists this information. Note that extra ferries always run during peak season.

When to Go

When to go is a decision of equal importance. The Aegean has a short, wet spring when walking, hiking, and mountain biking are extremely enjoyable activities, because the weather is pleasant but not too hot. The air is bright and clear — perfect for photography. However, travel arrangements can be difficult early in the season.

The traditional opening time for many hotels is the Orthodox Easter, although some do not open until the end of April. The ferry timetable runs on a winter (read curtailed) service until the first week in May.

Summer is long and hot, but the heat is tempered (or disguised) by the sometimes blustery Meltemi winds, which blow from the heart of central Asia, south through the Aegean. The summer season is also marked by an influx of backpackers and package vacationers from all across Europe. The islands are busy, but all facilities such as hotels and restaurants are open, and extra ferries and small boats (*caiques*) mean more opportunity to travel between islands.

Autumn is warm and the pace less frantic — perfect for such watching activities as the harvesting of the olives. By the middle of October, the season is over and many hotels and restaurants will close for the winter. Most of the staff you'll see in bars and hotels during the summer return to their homes on mainland Greece until the following year.

THE CYCLADES

Lying closest to Athens and the Attic peninsula, the Cyclades is the island chain most people would think of as typically Greek. Its islands have small fishing harbors replete with azure water, whitewashed houses with brightly colored trim, small domed chapels, and donkeys in their fields.

Originally named many centuries ago because its islands formed a circle or cyclos around the island of Delos — one of the most important sites in the ancient world — the Cyclades was first composed of a dozen islands. Twenty islands have since been added, making the Cyclades the largest of the Greek island groups.

You will definitely be sharing the main islands with many other visitors, although this has not yet spoiled their charms. For those who look for solitude, there are still quiet islands to be explored, off the beaten track.

Mykonos

A tiny, treeless rocky island regularly swept by summer winds has become one of the most popular vacation destinations in the Mediterranean. Why? Mykonos is a state of mind as well as a place. It's hedonistic and funky, and tolerant of alternative lifestyles. A mecca for gay travelers and nude sunbathers, Mykonos is also a trendy spot for the fabulous and well-connected, who come to shop in its designer boutiques (open almost around the clock) and go clubbing till sunrise.

Amazingly, the island retains its Greek character. The capital, Mykonos Town, is one of the most beautiful in the Aegean. The island happily caters to families in addition to single travelers, and backpackers as well as the wealthy. It offers a stepping stone to the sacred island of Delos, with all its archaeological treasures, yet has a variety of beaches for those who want to do little but soak in the sun.

☛ **Mykonos Town** is the only large settlement on the island. It's built on undulating land that radiates out from a fishing harbor where a small fleet still moors and

Petros the Pelican — mascot of Mykonos — pays a royal visit to some lucky local.

sells its catch. You will probably find the island mascot **Petros**, a pelican (the older Petros now has two young apprentices, both also called Petros) waddling among the boats, hoping for a fishy tidbit. Beside the port sits the quaint, round-domed **Paraportiani Church**, a favorite backdrop for fashion photographers.

Behind the port is a maze of narrow alleys and white-washed houses with overhanging balconies resplendent with potted plants and masses of bougainvillea. Art galleries, jewelers, and fashionable eateries can be found on every corner; but early in the morning, you'll have the streets to yourself, so enjoy every detail of the pretty Cycladic architecture.

Brightly painted doors hide cool courtyards and white paint outlines the stone pavements of the alleyways.

A small bay bounding the north side of town has Venetian balconies overhanging the water. Known as the **Alefkandra Quarter** or "Little Venice," it is the place to come for a sunset cocktail or dinner by the water's edge. From here, you'll get a full view of the line of five **windmills** that sit above the town.

Walking from the fishing harbor north toward the commercial port will take you past the small **Folklore Museum**, with exhibits of traditional Greek household items. Nearby, next to the southern bus station, is the **archaeological museum**. Among its many exhibits, there are funerary statues and other items from the island of Rhenia, the burial ground for the inhabitants of Delos.

> **Always wear appropriate dress when entering churches or monasteries.**
> **Men must wear long trousers and women must have shoulders and thighs covered.**

The interior of Mykonos is barren and dusty. The only buildings that break the monotony are the more than 300 small white chapels that dot the hillsides. Center of worship on the island is the red-roofed **Tourliani Monastery** with its 16th-century bell towers. It is situated at the center of the inland village of **Ano Mera,** whose small square makes a peaceful place for a leisurely lunch.

The beaches of Mykonos rival those of St. Tropez in their reputation for bohemian activities; however, there are enough stretches of sand and little coves that you can find somewhere that suits your own tastes. **Paradise Beach,** a clothing-optional beach, is probably the most famous, with nonstop music that lasts well into the early hours of the morning. **Super-Paradise,** in the next bay, is a gay, clothing-optional beach. Families head out to **Platis Gialos** or **Psarou,** but they can be crowded. Farther east, **Elia** and **Agia Anna** offer the promise of a little more space.

Highlights of the Aegean

There are many beautiful islands in the Aegean, but the following islands are particularly special.

Mykonos: Mykonos is the party and shopping capital of the Aegean. Beautiful Mykonos Town has archetypal Greek Cycladic architecture and a bohemian atmosphere, particularly in July and August when the young and the fabulous arrive, and almost anything goes.

Delos: One of the most important cities in the ancient world, Delos was a sacred island to the ancient Greeks and a commercial center for the Romans. Visit from another island, as there are no tourist facilities here.

Santorini: A powerful volcanic eruption around 1500 B.C. blew the center out of this island, leaving behind the largest caldera in the world. Honeycomb villages of brilliant white-washed houses, blue-domed churches clinging to edges of cliffs, and some of the most dramatic views in the world.

Kos: With Hellenic, Roman, Crusader, and Ottoman remains in one compact town and a network of other islands only a boat ride away, Kos is the perfect hub for island-hopping in the northern Dodecanese.

Patmos: In A.D. 95, John the Theologian (Evangelist in Greek) wrote the Book of Revelation on this small island. Explore the cave where he found divine inspiration, and visit the Monastery of St. John the Theologian founded in 1088, with its priceless collection of icons and religious jewelry. It is one of the holiest sites in the Greek Orthodox religion.

Delos

It is difficult to overestimate the importance of the sacred island of Delos during ancient times. According to Greek myth, it was the birthplace of Apollo, God of Light. It was believed to be free floating until Apollo's birth, after which huge columns rose up from the sea bed to anchor the island. Perhaps because of its geographical location at the center of the islands in the surrounding Cyclades chain, it also inspired the name for the island chain. (Cyclades, you may remember, comes from *cyclos*, or circle.) Delos was not only an important religious center, but also a major meeting point for trade between East and West during the Hellenistic and Roman eras. It was designated the home of the treasury of the Delian League in 480 B.C., an act which encouraged its growth as a center for banking and commerce. As a result, Delos is now one of the most important archaeological sites in the world. Its remains reflect its dual roles in ancient Greek life, a holy place and a center of trade.

Today, Delos has no modern settlement or tourist infrastructure. Visitors must travel here, by boat, as an excursion from a surrounding island, alighting at a small jetty beside the ancient port, now silted up. From here, the vista of the whole town can be seen, with a fine residential quarter to the right, and the remains of a series of magnificent temples to the left. The temples were the last stop on a long pilgrimage for ancient Greek believers. Here, you could make offerings to the god Apollo at his birthplace, or consult the powerful oracle in residence.

From the ferry jetty, turn left and walk down the **Sacred Way**. In the distance, you will see a fine palm tree, a symbol of Apollo's birthplace. Surrounding it are the remains of the **Sacred Lake**, drained in the 1920s to prevent mosquitoes from breeding in the stagnant water. Walking through the site toward the palm tree will take you past the **Sanctuary of Apollo**, comprising a series of once fine colonnaded stoas and temples, including one to Apollo's sister, Artemis.

A number of lion statues, **the Terrace of the Lions**, form a honor guard on the approach to the sacred lake. They are perhaps the most photographed symbol of Delos, and are believed to date from the seventh century B.C. Their numbers have dwindled over the centuries from 16 to only 5. Today, an attempt is being made to recreate the statues in their prime, with modern materials. At present, only one is in its natural aged state.

On higher ground behind the lake is the **Museum of Delos**. Although it has the dour look of a barracks building, it houses many of the finest statuary and artifacts found at

Photo op! The five windmills of Alefkandra in Mykonos Town reveal a Cycladic scene of rustic simplicity.

the site, and they bring to life the bare bones of the temple buildings and houses. Fine pottery and exquisite jewelry show that daily life was enhanced by quality possessions, which were taken for granted by the population.

To the left of the temple area is perhaps one of the most exciting parts of Delos, the **Theater Quarter**, although the theater itself (third century B.C.) is not the highlight of the site. It is the labyrinth of family houses in its shadow that brings the city to life. Streets that have felt the footfalls of ancient Greeks and Romans still lead to the front doors of their homes and shops. Some are meager square boxes, but behind a number of strong stone walls, magnificent homes are revealed. Interior courtyards were beautified by some of the most ornate mosaic floors and wall frescoes in the ancient world. Search out the **House of Dionysos** and the **House of the Trident** with their

simple floor patterns, and the **House of Dolphins** and the **House of Masks** for more elaborate examples, including Dionysos riding a panther, on the floor of the House of Masks. The **House of Cleopatra** is also worthy of note, named for the lady of the house who left behind headless statues of herself and her husband, Dioskourides. The statues *in situ* are reproductions — the originals sit in

Ancient history, good as new. Headless statues in the House of Cleopatra, Delos.

the Delos Museum. Behind the Theater Quarter is an area with a number of shrines dedicated to foreign gods, an indication of the numerous cultures that influenced Delos. Syrian and Egyptian gods were worshipped here.

Above the town, the slopes of **Mount Kynthos** rise to a height of 112 m (367 ft), offering a view across the whole site. The climb — along a narrow and sometimes steep path — will lead to scant remains of third-century B.C. temples, although the site was occupied as early as the Stone Age.

Lying a few hundred meters to the west, the island of **Rhenia** was both a birthplace for Delians and their burial ground. Delos was a sacred island and its soil had to be kept pure; therefore, birth and death were prohibited human activities. Even today this ancient code is still being kept by modern archaeologists. Funerary artifacts found here are displayed in Mykonos.

Andros

The nearest Cyclades island to the Greek mainland, Andros is a short ferry ride from the port of Rafina, and is therefore very popular with Athenians for weekends and summer vacations. Wealthy shipping families own large houses along the coast and in the hills, which are more ver-

> Good morning, evening
> *kaliméra/kalispéra*

dant than those of other islands in the group, and its red soil contrasts with the dull earth of Mykonos or Paros.

The major port of **Gavrion** on the west coast serves the whole island, but the main town is **Chora** (which simply means "town," and is often used on islands with only one main settlement). Off the tourist route, on the east coast of the island, it is also known as **Andros Town**. Much of Chora has remained unchanged for decades, as Athenian weekenders have refurbished the charming old townhouses, and it has a very genteel air.

The cultural heart of Andros owes much to the generosity of the Goulandris shipping family. They funded the **Modern Art Museum,** just to the north of the main square, which features the work of a selection of European modernist painters. They were also instrumental in the creation of the **archaeological museum** that houses the Hermes of Andros, a second-century copy of a statue originally sculpted by Praxiteles.

The main resort is **Batsi** on the west coast, just south of Gavrion. The small center still retains vestiges of its heritage as a fishing village, but modern hotels and apartments have been built on the outskirts.

The Monastery of Zoodohos Pighi (Life-giving Spring) lies in the hills above Batsi and guards what is considered to be the most sacred of several freshwater springs found on the island.

Tinos

Tinos is a surprise because it is a center of Roman Catholic worship in an Orthodox land. This is in part because the island remained under Catholic Venetian rule far longer than other islands in the Aegean — from 1207 to 1714 — but also because it was the scene of a blessed miracle, ensuring its fame throughout the Catholic community in Greece. In 1823, a nun from the Convent of Kechrovouni had a dream in which the Virgin Mary told her that a sacred icon could be found in land nearby. The nun went out and found the portrait just as her dream had foretold. Since that time, the icon has been held responsible for many feats of healing, giving Tinos the epithet "Lourdes of Greece." The island is a delight, because it has few foreign visitors and retains its strong Greek character.

The capital of the island, **Tinos Town,** houses the icon in the **Panagia Evangelistria**, a church that sits at the top of a gentle slope rising up from the port 1 km (0.6 miles) away. The icon has a powerful influence over pilgrims, who crawl up the church steps on their hands and knees to pray for divine intervention. Two major festivals, Assumption Day on 15 August and Annunciation Day on 25 March, see thousands of believers crawling up the hill from the port to worship the icon. Don't travel to the island at either of these times without a reservation.

Worshippers light candles in the Panagia Evangelistria, Tinos Town.

Travel into the countryside and you'll soon see how hilly Tinos is. Hundreds of terraces cover the hillsides, giving them a textured look. Today, many lie overgrown and unused, but during Venetian times, they brimmed with crops and grew fodder for livestock. They are made accessible by thousands of narrow donkey tracks, which are used by hikers and ramblers.

Scattered across the land are hundreds of **dovecotes,** which were introduced throughout the Aegean by the

Venetians, who enjoyed pigeon as a part of their diet. On other islands, the towers have been allowed to decay, but on Tinos they stand proud, many with birds still in residence. Some of the most accessible can be found near the village of **Tarabados**, 8 km (13 miles) north of Tinos Town.

The ground rises dramatically behind Tinos Town to a rocky peak called **Exobourgo**. Here the remains of a massive Venetian fortress destroyed by invading Ottoman forces can be found. Wander, at your own risk, among the walls, crumbling turrets, and caves, and look out toward the surrounding islands of Mykonos and Andros. In the shadow of the peak is a network of villages, unspoiled both by the influence of tourists and the excesses of modern life. One of the prettiest, **Dyo Chorio**, has fresh spring water fountains which are still used by hill farmers to collect water for their homes. Village households still wash their laundry in these waters.

The central section of Tinos has little of interest, but make your way over the hills to the pretty village of **Pyrgos**, famed for its school of marble carving. The village, nestled into a narrow valley, is one of the prettiest in the Aegean. A number of craftsmen have studios fronting onto the narrow streets. From Pyrgos, head down to the fishing port of **Panormos** 3 km (2 miles) away, where you can enjoy delicious fresh fish at one of the many *tavernas*.

How Many Doors?

The Church of 100 Doors has in fact only 99 known doors. Local folklore states that when the one hundredth door is found, it will signal the resurgence of the Byzantine Orthodox Empire and the return of its first city, Constantinople (now Istanbul in Turkey) into Greek hands.

Sifnos

In ancient times, Sifnos was famed for its gold and silver deposits. The island's treasury, stored at Delphi (the most important sanctuary in ancient Greece) was said to be the richest of the many deposited there. In more recent times, wealth has passed the island by, but it still produces some jewelry and has a reputation for particularly fine pottery, which can be seen outside the workshops drying in the sun. The island also claims some 365 churches and monasteries nestled among its abundant olive groves.

The main port, **Kamares**, lies 5 km (3 miles) from the capital **Apollonia**, and its sister town **Artemon** (both named for the brother and sister god and goddess of ancient Greek mythology). The oldest continually occupied settlement on the island is **Kastro**, where most of the buildings date from the 14th century and were laid out in a circular pattern atop a rocky outcrop 100 m (300 ft) above the east coast. The town is a fascinating mixture of crumbling grandeur and renovated splendor. An **archaeological museum** is housed in a building of Venetian origin and contains finds from the Mycenaean and Archaic periods.

The main beaches of Sifnos lie on the south coast. **Platis Gialos** is popular with a range of bars and tavernas, but Vathi is perhaps the most visually stunning, with the now de-consecrated 17th-century **Hrysopighi Monastery** set on a small offshore island reached by a bridge.

Paros and Antiparos

A veritable Grand Central Station of ferry services, Paros is an island with something for almost everyone. Across a narrow channel sits Antiparos (translated as "opposite Paros"), with a main settlement which takes you back to the Greek Islands of twenty years ago.

The capital of Paros, **Parikia**, serves the port, and although it is extremely busy throughout the peak season, it still retains the feel of a Greek town. Away from the port, a maze of narrow streets disguise the remains of a *kastro*, or castle, dating from the 13th century, which recycled marble from Greek and Roman temples on the island.

To the left of the port, beside the new medical center, is the **Panagia Ekatontapiliani**, known as the **Church of 100 Doors.** The present buildings are based around a fourth-century structure that is said to have been commissioned by St. Helen, mother of Constantine the Great (founder of Constantinople and the leader who converted the Roman Empire to Christianity), and the sixth-century chapel uses columns from an earlier Roman temple.

Nearby, the **archaeological museum** has a section of the Parian Chronicles, a history of ancient Greece enscribed on marble slabs, along with other examples of Paros marble, which was coveted throughout the ancient world for its fine translucence.

Leave Parikia behind and Paros has a number of villages to explore. In the north, **Naoussa** has one of the prettiest fishing harbors in the Mediterranean. Although popular with visitors, it has not lost its traditional industry. Boats in daily use lie within feet of the fashionable bars and restaurants. It's no surprise that the harbor has some of the best seafood restaurants in the Aegean, including several traditional Greek ouzeries. To the west of Naoussa is **Kolymbithres**, a growing resort whose beaches are surrounded by strange rock features that are folded by immense natural forces and eroded by the wind. The resort has a large park featuring water slides and a children's play area.

Along the eastern coastline are several fine beaches with perfect windsurfing conditions in their wide, shallow bays.

Nest with a view — Greek pigeons sit pretty in their custom-made dovecotes.

The World Windsurfing Championships have been held here in August for the last several years. **Golden Beach** is perfect for soaking up the sun and watching the sport. Farther along the east coast is the pretty port of **Piso Livadi**.

The interior of the island has a number of interesting attractions. **Lefkes** village occupies high ground in the interior, and its narrow streets are perfect places to explore. Look out for the remains of a marble-covered **Byzantine road** (fourth- to century–14th-century) that once connected Lefkes with the nearby village of Karampoli down in the valley.

Near the village of **Marathi** you will find the ancient marble quarries that sent stone to all parts of the Greek and Roman empires. The stone was mined rather than cut from the surface, and the tunnels can be explored with a flashlight. The building remains you'll see once housed French workmen who came here in 1844 to cut marble for Napoleon's tomb in the Hôtel des Invalides in Paris.

If you visit Paros in July or August, be sure to take a trip to **Petaloudes** or the Valley of the Butterflies south of Parikia, a breeding ground for giant tiger moths. Here you can see tiger moths clinging to the leaves of trees, sometimes in vast numbers.

Until 5,000 years ago, **Antiparos** was attached to Paros, but seismic activity and climatic change have produced a narrow sea channel with several tiny islands between the two. Antiparos can be reached by a 20-minute ferry ride from Parikia, or a five-minute car ferry trip from the small port of Pounda on Paros's western coast.

The town of Antiparos seems to move at a slower pace than Parikia; in fact, the town can be almost somnolent out of season. At its heart is a **Venetian kastro** that still retains original dwelling houses along its interior walls.

The main attractions on the island are the **caves** under the mountain of Agios Ilias in the south. The interior is cavernous, but the caves have suffered

Unfinished business — portal to a planned Temple of Apollo, sixth century B.C.

from centuries of vandalism. The number of steps built down into the interior means that it is unsuitable for the infirm or those with heart problems.

Naxos

The largest island in the Cyclades, Naxos is a place of contrasts. It has ranges of barren hills and mountains as well as green fertile valleys that produce grapes and olives in abundance. The island has a long history; its marble deposits were coveted around the ancient world. In fact, the Lions of Delos were made from Naxos marble. The wonderful beaches along the western coast were, until recently, a secret, but they have now been discovered. Tourism has grown over the last ten years.

The capital of Naxos, **Hora,** sits on the western coastline and is served by a rather breezy but extremely busy port. There is a wide promenade along the seafront with cafés and restaurants, but the heart of the magnificent old town lies just above this, overlooking the harbor. It comprises a labyrinth of alleyways and narrow streets around a **Venetian citadel,** which caps the highest point. Small Byzantine churches sit on street corners, side by side with family homes. The church of **Panagia Theoskepastos** houses a fine 14th-century icon, and the **Catholic Cathedral** has a tenth-century Madonna and Child. Next door to the cathedral is the **archaeological museum** with finds from every era of Naxos's long history.

On a rocky promontory beside the town is the site of the **Temple of Apollo,** dating from the sixth century B.C. It was planned as the largest temple in the Aegean, but was never completed. Only the giant portal, 5.5 m (18 ft) tall, was in place when work stopped, but it gives an indication of how immense the whole task would have been.

Santorini dreaming...white-washed buildings tipped with blue above an azure sea.

The interior of Naxos offers a range of environments not found on other islands of the Aegean. Fertile valleys with precious water supplies offer a cool and fragrant break from the heat of the towns and beaches. The valley between the towns of **Chalki** and **Filoti** (known as the **Tragea Valley**) is perhaps the most beautiful, and easily reached by bus from Hora. Ancient olive groves play host to donkeys and herds of goats, and low-growing vines cover the ground under tall Cypress trees — the archetypal Greek landscape. The heart of Chalki hides a Venetian tower and the whole valley has a number of small Byzantine chapels.

Filoti sits in the shadow of **Mount Zas**, a treeless brown rock rising from the green valley below. Although you can't climb to the summit, there are beautiful walks or cycle paths on its lower slopes, with caves to explore and cooling streams to enjoy.

Traveling north out of the Tragea Valley past villages seemingly clinging to the valley sides, **Keramoti**, **Koronos**, and **Korinada** are all fascinating places to explore. All give glimpses of traditional family life. A small resort on the northern coast, **Apollon**, holds a fascinating artifact from the past. A giant block of marble, formed into a *kouros* (male statue) over 2,600 years ago lies prostrate on the ground. The marble cracked before the figure was finished and it was abandoned where it lay.

The best sandy beaches of Naxos lie on the sheltered west coast to the south of Chora. **Agia Anna**, and the long sandy spit of **Agios Prokopios** are two of the most popular.

Santorini

The island of Santorini (Thira) is one of the must-see places of the world, for no other reason than because it frames the earth's largest volcanic caldera. Santorini looked exactly like many of the other islands in the Cyclades until around 1500 B.C., when a massive eruption of its volcano carried the whole interior of the island high into the atmosphere, changing the climate of the earth for years afterwards. In place of land came water, surging in to fill the 11-km (7-mile) long void and causing massive tidal waves around the Mediterranean Sea.

What remains today is the outer rim of the original circular island. Sheer cliffs up to 300 m (984 ft) high bound the caldera, and a number of whitewashed settlements nestle along their crests, looking from a distance like icing melting down the sides of a cake.

Another section of the original island sits to the west. **Thirasia** now has separate settlements that can be visited by ferry from Santorini. In the center of the caldera are two low-lying areas of land that appeared after the 1500 B.C. eruption: **Nea Kameni** and **Palea Kameni.** Because the volcano is still active — although dormant at present — these areas continue to grow, and experience earthquakes. The last major one, in 1956, inflicted a great deal of damage to the towns on the main island.

Once on Santorini, visitors are usually surprised to see, beyond the high steep caldera to the east, coastal plains that are covered in a blanket of vines. Indeed, more than 100,000 bottles of wine are produced here every year and shipped worldwide.

The main town of the island is **Fira**, set atop the high cliffs in the center of the long interior curve. Its buildings tumble down toward the water with stunning views. A narrow cobbled trail of 587 steps leads from the town to the small port below, now the domain of a fleet of donkeys that wait to carry cruise ship passengers into town. For those who would prefer a quicker method, there is a cable car that wings you from sea level to the cliffs in a couple of minutes. Most commercial ferries arrive at the new port of **Athinios** farther along the coast.

Fira is a shopper's paradise, a series of narrow alleys where you can wander free from the fear of traffic, although keep your eyes and ears open for donkeys. You can buy anything from a reproduction icon to a genuine Fabergé egg, plus jewelry of the finest quality and designer clothing by the most desirable names. Find a spot for a drink at sunset (which has to be one of the most spectacular on earth).

Is This the Lost Civilization of Atlantis?

The myth of Atlantis lives on as strongly as ever. This most enlightened society of peaceful and fulfilled people who lived with all they desired was destroyed by a natural disaster of unprecedented ferocity.

Although no one can be sure that Atlantis ever existed, some experts say that the story fits the facts of the ancient Santorini eruption, and that the remains at Akrotiri may be the site of this most perfect of cities.

Among the boutiques and bars are two places of cultural interest. The **archaeological museum** on a square next to the cable car station (a new building is under construction near the main bus station, which will eventually house the collection) features pottery and other artifacts found on the island. The **Megaron Gyzi Museum** to the north of the cable car station is housed in a beautiful 17th-century fortified house. Most exciting of its varied collections is a display of photographs showing island scenes from before the devastating 1956 earthquake.

Black and blue: dramatic color combinations at Perissa volcanic beach, Santorini.

Fira is beautiful, but it can get oppressive when visitors crowd the narrow streets. A little way north is another smaller town where the pace is less frantic. **Ia** (pronounced Oya), set on the northern cliffs, became home to a number of artists early on, and it maintains a more bohemian atmosphere than Fira. There are many homes built into the hillsides; some have been converted into art galleries and shops selling collectibles. The architecture is typical of the Cyclades, and the buildings' multicolored façades make it one of the most photographed villages in the world.

Aside from the stunning views, Santorini has much more to show its visitors. In the center of the island is the village of **Pirgos,** with the remains of a Venetian fortress at its heart. On a rocky bluff beyond the village you will find the 17th-century **Monastery of Profitis Ilias.** As the road climbs toward the entrance, you'll pass fields full of Santorini's famed tomatoes growing on the steep slopes. The monastery is only open when the priests inside take liturgies (mornings and early evenings), but it is well worth taking the time to visit. Pride of place goes to a 15th-century icon of the prophet Elijah. The monastery also has a museum, which conveys the flavor of monastic life along with icons and manuscripts. Unfortunately, the hilltop is also shared by the Greek military, and it bristles with satellite and digital technology, prohibiting photography of the beautiful panorama.

On the northern slopes of this rocky outcropping is the site of the ancient capital of the island, also called **Thira,** which dates from the third century B.C. (when the Aegean was under Ptolemaic rule). The site sprawls over a wide area, but unfortunately, some remains are in poor condition, a situation which causes the site to close intermittently because of the danger of falling masonry. Check with the tourist information authorities in Fira before setting out.

In the south of the island is one of the most important ancient sites in the Mediterranean. Near the modern village of **Akrotiri,** a complete city dating from before 2000 B.C. was discovered. It was covered by several feet of ash during the eruption of c.1500 B.C., but unlike the tragic city of Pompeii in Italy, no human remains have been found. This has led scientists to believe that the population escaped before the disaster took place.

Since 1967, the site has been painstakingly excavated to give a picture of daily life before the great eruption. A society of complexity and sophistication has been unveiled, one that had urban planning, heating, sanitation,

and a standard script. However, much of the beautiful art-
work found here is, for the moment, in the archaeological

Off the Beaten Track: Milos, Syros, Amorgos & the Back Islands

Adventurous travelers may enjoy visiting these out-of-the
way islands, which rarely show up on Aegean itineraries.

Milos: This island is home to the famous statue the Venus
de Milo, which now rests in the Louvre museum in Paris. In
the Bronze Age, Milos was important for its seam of hard
obsidian rock (vitreous lava), a material which was used to
make early tools. Today, the island's unusual rock forma-
tions continue to attract geologists from around the world.

Syros: Capital of the Cyclades, this small island has one
of the few truly administrative towns in the Aegean. Er-
moupolis is a cultural center, with grand public buildings,
large squares, and an urbane population comprised of civil
servants and professionals working standard Greek office
hours — very different from the small towns of other islands, where industry involves catering to the tourists more
than anything else.

Amorgos: Famed for the starkly beautiful Byzantine
Monastery of Hozoviotissa, which was built against a verti-
cal rock face. This island, one of the most easterly islands in
the Cyclades, also has the smallest church in Greece (it can
accommodate only two worshippers).

The Back Islands: A series of five tiny islands that sit off
the southeastern coast of Naxos. Donoussa, Iraklia, Shi-
noussa, and Koufonisi each have a population of no more
than 200 people, making them true island retreats. Keros is
uninhabited, but during the Cycladic era (the third millennium B.C.), it was the home of many fine funerary artisans.
Most of the museum pieces in Athens dating from this period were found here. For this reason, it is off-limits to visitors.

museum in Athens. The site is still an active dig and new discoveries are being made all the time. The remains, which include streets with houses and pretty communal squares, have been placed under a protective, corrugated roof that gets hot and crowded, so try to visit as early in the day as possible.

The beaches of Santorini are made of fine black or red volcanic sand, which heats to a ferocious temperature in the summer sun. **Kamari** and **Perissa** are growing resorts with a range of hotels, bars, and restaurants. Both make pleasant retreats after a day of sightseeing in Fira or Akrotiri.

Some of the best views of Santorini are from the water. Try taking a trip around the caldera, with stops at the new volcanic islands of Nea and Palea Kameni. Allow time in Thirasia to explore Santorini's smaller sibling islands.

Ios

Ios is hands-down the party island of the Aegean; its bars and clubs boom out the latest dance tunes 24 hours a day. Traditionally a poor island, the native population has happily embraced the new seasonal lifestyle that has brought them prosperity, and the old ways have almost completely disappeared.

Arriving by boat gives you splendid views of the magnificent unspoiled, treeless landscape, which bears scant evidence of the hand of man. Only the southeastern corner has any real development, and the road system comprises less than 10 km (16 miles) from the pretty, narrow streets of Chora, the island's only town, to the beach at **Milopotamos** in the neighboring bay. Milopotamos is one of the best and busiest beaches in the Aegean. This leaves a whole island to explore on foot, or by 4-wheel-drive vehicle. Residents of Ios will tell you that an **ancient tomb** in the north of the island is that of Homer, author of *The Odyssey* and *The Iliad.* (His mother was born on Ios.) Unfortunately, no positive proof has ever corroborated the claim.

THE DODECANESE

The Dodecanese islands take their name from the Greek phrase *dodeka nisi,* meaning twelve islands, although the group incorporates far more than one dozen in its number. The islands did not become part of Greece until 1947. From 1912 to 1947, they were ruled by Italy; before that, they were part of the

The minaret of Loggia Mosque with Hippocrates Tree (to the right) in Kos.

Ottoman Empire. The major islands exhibit faded remains of a Muslim influence, though this was just one of several cultures to leave its mark on the islands.

Kos

Now the second most populated island in the Dodecanese, Kos has seen human settlement since ancient times. With safe harbors and wide fertile plains, it could both protect and feed its people. Today it is very popular with package vacationers, particularly high-spirited young Europeans. Try to visit early or late in the season to avoid the crowds and their worst excesses.

Major Attractions of the Aegean

Important details about major attractions on the Aegean Islands follow. The attractions are listed in the order they appear in this guide.

Delos Island Sacred temple site and trading port throughout the ancient Greek and Roman empires. Open daily except Monday 8am–3pm; entrance fee; involves a ferry ride from Mykonos. (see page 32).

Ancient Akrotiri, Santorini Remains of the Minoan city dating from before 2000 B.C. Open daily except Monday 8am–8pm (winter until dusk); entrance fee. (see page 48).

Castle of the Knights of St. John, Kos Fifteenth-century castle. Open daily except Monday 8am–2:30pm; entrance fee. (see page 53).

The Asclepium, Kos A medical center dating from the fourth century B.C. Open daily except Monday 8:30am–3:30pm, later in summer; entrance fee. (see page 54).

Monastery of St. John the Theologian and Convent of the Apocalypse, Patmos Sites of pilgrimage where John the Theologian (Evangelist in Greek) wrote the Book of Revelation. Generally open daily from 8am–1pm; no entrance fee (see page 56).

Castle of Mytilini, Lesvos Venetian and Ottoman castle. Open daily except Monday 9am–3pm; entrance fee. (see page 63).

Archaeological Museum of Mytilini, Lesvos One of the finest collections in Greece, with finds from all eras of this cultural center's history. Open daily except Monday 8:30am–1:30pm and 5pm–9pm; entrance fee. (see page 63).

The Petrified Forest, Lesvos Ancient sequoia trees turned to stone. Open daily 9am–8pm; entrance fee. (see page 65).

Nea Moni Monastery, Chios Byzantine monastery in a beautiful setting. Open daily 8am–1pm, 4pm–8pm; no entrance fee (see page 67).

Kos Town on the western coast is the main settlement, and a fascinating place to explore. Settled for many centuries, it suffered an earthquake in 1933 that damaged much of the modern town center, but allowed Italian archaeologists to excavate a large section of the **Roman city** which lay directly underneath. Today it is possible to walk through the old *agora* (marketplace) and stroll along Roman roads.

Later, after the fall of Jerusalem, the town became a stronghold of the Knights of St. John. In the 15th century, they built the **Castle of the Knights of St. John** at the water's edge. It still forms an impressive backdrop for photographs of Mandraki Harbor, and is filled with historical "litter," including carved marble plaques, statuary, and cannons.

Ottoman forces ousted the knights in 1522, and evidence of their stay can be found just inland from the castle. The minaret of the **Loggia Mosque**, built in the 18th century and the largest on Kos, now stands silent and closed, but it is matched by a number of smaller examples throughout town, some still in use by the small Muslim population.

Beside the mosque — in fact, almost overshadowing it — is a large plane tree. Its branches extend so far that it has had to be supported for many years by a framework of scaffolding. The local people will tell you that this is the **Hippocrates Tree**, under which the father of medicine, a native of the island, lectured to his students over 2,500 years ago. Sadly, although the tree has been proved to be among the oldest in Europe, most experts believe that it is only 2,000 years old and therefore not of Hippocrates's era.

In the main square of the town (walk inland from the mosque on the south side of the agora) is the **archaeological museum,** which features finds from ancient Kos, including mosaics and domestic utensils. On the outskirts of town, on E Grigorou Street, is a small **Roman Odeon** or theater, used in summer for performances. Nearby is **Casa Romana,** a Roman villa recreated in every detail. It really brings to life the daily routines of a wealthy Roman family.

If you don't want to walk around town, a small motorized train runs past all the major sites. It operates several times a day during the summer.

Four kilometers (2 ½ miles) outside Kos Town are the remains of a medical school founded in the fourth century B.C., just after the death of Hippocrates. The **Asclepium** was a major center of healing. Many of the largest remains date from the Roman, rather than the Classical Greek era, and the site was damaged by the Knights of St. John when they removed marble from it to build their castle in Kos Town. The main Doric temple rested on the upper level of the three terraces that make up the site. There are fine views across to Turkey from here.

Resorts outside Kos Town include **Kardamena** on the south coast, a young, energetic resort; **Tigaki** on the north coast, a quiet resort more suited to couples and families; and Kamari, which

Interior courtyard,
Monastery of St. John
the Theologian.

sits the farthest from Kos Town. All offer a selection of hotels, bars, and restaurants.

The flat landscape, especially in the east, is ideal for cycling, where you can get away and explore such inland villages as **Pyli** (and the older Paleo Pyli high in the hills), **Asfendiou,** and **Kefalos,** with the last working windmill on the island. Here you can still find a quiet spot to enjoy authentic Greek island life.

Patmos

This small, barren island in the northern Dodecanese may have remained the deserted outpost it once was, had it not been for a decision in the first century A.D. to use it as a penal colony for political and religious dissidents. It was here in 95 A.D. that one resident received divine inspiration in the form of an apocalyptic vision while he sat in his small cave high above the harbor. The words which John the Theologian (Evangelist in Greek) recorded became the Book of Revelation (Apocalypse in Greek), the last book of the New Testament.

In 1098, the Byzantine Emperor ceded land on the island to a monk, Christodoulos, who founded a monastery here in honor of the saint. It soon became a place of contemplation, learning, and pilgrimage — a role it still performs for thousands of believers to the present day.

Since there is no airport on the island, all visitors must arrive at the port, **Skala**, where most of the hotels are located and all commercial activity is carried out. Despite the number of visitors passing through, Skala is still a Greek village at heart, with a number of traditional tavernas to be found in the streets around the small main square. A new yacht basin to the east allows safe harbor for independent travelers.

Everyone who arrives at the port can look up and see their first view of the **Monastery of St. John the Theologian**, surrounded by the town of **Chora** atop a nearby hill. The monastery was built at a tumultuous time in Christian history and its design was based on that of a castle, to act as a protection of the faith and its treasures, as well as for worship. It stands high above myriad whitewashed walls.

Historically, a narrow cobbled track transported pilgrims from the port to the monastery, either on foot or by donkey. The path still exists, and in the cool of the early morning, it is a pleasant uphill walk. Others can take one of the regular buses or a taxi for the ten-minute ride.

Halfway up the hill is the **Convent of the Apocalypse**, at the site of the cave where St. John received his divine revelation. Now tended by nuns, it is regarded as holy ground (follow the same rules of dress expected at other holy places). The small **Cave of St. Anne** has a silver band where it is said St. John laid his head each night, and a simple rock ledge is said to have been his desk. Two chapels now grace the grounds.

On reaching Chora, you will need to walk through the pedestrian-only town to reach the monastery. The streets have an almost eerie emptiness, although in summer small kittens scamper away as you approach, disappearing into cracks in the thick, high walls. Eventually the signposts will lead to the strong stone archway that signals the entrance to the Monastery of St. John.

Immediately on entering the cobbled main courtyard, you will find a small church on the left, built on the site of an ancient temple of Artemis. Inside you will find the marble sarcophagus of the monastery's founder Christodoulos and icons that date from as early as 1190. Behind the chapel is the 11th-century refectory where it is possible to gain an insight into the daily lives of the generations of monks who made this monastery their home. The utilitarian communal tables and simple decorations offered no distractions from their serious vocation.

Take the staircase in the eastern corner of the courtyard to find the treasury, which displays only a fraction of the wealth

Off the Beaten Track in the Dodecanese

Astypalaea: A butterfly-shaped island, set in the sea out toward the Cyclades, Astypalaea is still difficult to reach, lying off the main tourist routes. Having been adopted by French visitors, the bars and cafés of the main towns and resorts offer a certain *je ne sais quoi*.

Kastellorizo: The most easterly of the Greek islands, Kastellorizo sits in the shadow of the Turkish coast. It has another name, Meghisti, which means "large," yet it is the smallest inhabited Greek island. At the beginning of the 20th century it was thriving, making a living from shipping. Since that time, bad luck and depopulation (only a couple hundred people returned after World War II) has created a legacy of faded glory. Elegant townhouses now compete with the crumbling Crusader castle and the ancient Lycian tomb above the town.

Nissyros: The Greek God of the Sea, Poseidon, was in conflict with Polyvotis, a Titan. When Poseidon discovered Polyvotis in the water just south of Kos, he took some rock from the island and crushed his foe beneath it. This crushed rock became the island of Nissyros.

With a dormant volcano at its heart, the cry of the Titan is still said to be heard in the hissing hot springs and the occasional murmur from the depths of the earth.

accumulated by the monastery. Beautifully displayed are a range of icons dating from the 12th century, silver altar pieces and bejeweled vestments. The monastery received bequests from nobility throughout the Orthodox world, and was not averse to making money from commerce, particularly shipping. In this way, it amassed vast fortunes still kept under lock and key.

The library was once one of the most important in the Byzantine world. Large numbers of volumes were evacuated from here before the fall of Constantinople, comprising the best in early Christian decorated manuscripts and books of the Bible. However, the library is only open to scholars and requires prior written permission for research.

Despite the importance of the monastery, a great deal of ordinary life can be seen around Patmos. Small holdings abound, and traditional houses sit low on the treeless hillsides. The beaches on the northern coastline beyond the village of **Kambos** are said to be the best, although some are difficult to reach. Most accessible is **Lampis Bay**, with a couple of good tavernas. South of Skala is the small resort of **Grikos Bay**.

Kalymnos

For centuries, the natives of Kalymnos were renowned for their diving prowess. They developed it in order to harvest the sponges that grew abundantly in the seas all around the island. However, the early 20th century saw several catastrophic changes that ruined the commercial sponge industry on Kalymnos. Many families emigrated to the United States and Australia to make new lives, and the natural population dropped dramatically.

Although the traditional industry is a great deal smaller than it once was, tourism has taken up the slack; in summer,

Kalymnos is busy with vacationing families from several European countries.

Kalymnos has a barren interior with dramatic cliffs and caves all around its coastline. The capital, **Pothia,** is a splash of bright color climbing a hillside on the south coast. With a population of around 11,000, it is one of the largest towns in the Dodecanese and is the major port on the island. Today, a small fleet of sponge fishermen still sets sail every summer, although the crop remains in decline. The statue of a mermaid sits on the breakwater as a lucky omen for the sailors, and families turn out to perform a religious ceremony to guide and protect their loved ones.

Yet another perfect picture...Here, the harborfront of Mytilini, capital of Lesvos.

The black icon of Lesvos's Taxiarhis Monastery is believed to be made of soil wet with the blood of slaughtered monks.

Beyond Pothia, the castle (Pera Kastro) at **Horio**, the medieval capital, is clearly visible. The beach resorts of **Mirties** and **Massouri** on the west coast take the bulk of visitors. Massouri has fleets of boats that offer day trips to the island of **Telendos** only a mile or so offshore.

To the east of Pothia, the road leads to a fertile fruit-producing valley near **Vathi**. In the clear waters offshore are the remains of an Italian naval vessel sunk by British forces in World War II.

Karpathos

Karpathos is a rugged and wild island lying between Rhodes and Crete, almost at the foot of the Aegean. During the last one hundred years a large percentage of the population, tired of fighting the hard economic conditions, emigrated to the United States.

The remaining population is based mainly in the south, around the capital, **Pigadia,** which is relatively modern by Greek standards (built since the mid-19th century). Around it lie fields of fertile soil supporting orchards and grain crops.

The middle of the island has mountains that rise over 1,200 m (4,050 ft), separating the northern part of the island, and protecting it from the effects of development in the south. From Pigadia to the small southern port of **Diafani,** where vehicles find it difficult to travel, boats move people and goods. From here it is a steep journey up to the village of **Olimbos,** which still holds fast to its traditional way of life. The houses are built

| Yes *ne* |
| No *óchi* |

to a long-standing design and are filled with embroidery, lace, and crochet work. Older women in the village still dress in colorful traditional costumes which the younger women and children wear on feast days.

The remaining parts of the north, although enticing, are difficult to explore. One exception is the hike north from Olimbos to the **shrine to St. John the Baptist at Vrykounda**, site of a major island festival on 29 August every year.

THE EASTERN AEGEAN

Close to western Turkey, three large islands lie aligned from north to south: Lesvos, Chios, and Samos. These islands, known as the eastern Aegean Islands, have been at the forefront of waves of invasion from the east. Phoenicians and Persians came here to attack the kingdoms of the ancient Greek mainland; later, the Ottomans used this region as a base when they forced the Venetians and the Genoese to flee back to their homelands. The populations of all three islands played a major role in the fight for Greek statehood at the

Pride of Lesvos — these prehistoric sequoias at the Petrified Forest are a must-see.

beginning of the 19th century. They also saw a wave of Greek immigrants from the Turkish mainland during and after the proclamation of the Turkish state in 1923.

Despite hostile feelings in the past, relations between Greece and Turkey are now genial, at least on a day-to-day basis. One of the most exciting facets of a trip to the eastern Aegean Islands is the possibility of taking a day trip to Turkey, where you can experience the contrasting (though sometimes surprisingly similar) culture, and see the majestic ancient archaeological sites of old Asia Minor.

Lesvos

Lesvos is the third-largest Aegean island (after Crete and Evia), and it has a long and independent cultural tradition. Music, poetry, and dance have always been important parts of the island's identity. It was the birthplace of the ancient poet Sappho, said by Homer to be the tenth muse, and the musician Alcaeus, the father of Greek music. The Ottoman Sultans held Lesvos in high esteem for its fertile lands and the fine olive oil produced here, however, following the creation of the Turkish state in the 1920s, it lost its main market and became a backwater of the Aegean.

The island's capital is **Mytilini** (and you may sometimes hear Greeks call the island Mytilini, rather than Lesvos). A trading town and port, its main shopping street, **Ormos Ermou,** still throngs with the energy of an eastern bazaar. Fine 18th-century villas can be found along the seafront, both north of the port and south toward the airport. The villas were built for Ottoman traders and overseers, but were abandoned in the exchange of populations in the 1920s.

But the most impressive structure is the **medieval castle** built atop Roman, Hellenistic, and more ancient settlements. One of the largest fortifications in the Aegean, the interior Venetian walls were later expanded by the Ottomans. Resting in the shadow of the castle walls is the **Lesvos Archaeological Museum**, with one of the finest collections of artifacts in Greece. A new, air-conditioned, state-of-the-art building has been added on to the original museum, a fine old mansion. Throughout the two structures there are finds from all eras of Lesvos's history. Intricate mosaics depicting scenes from Menender's comedies are displayed beautifully, with clear glass tile

---

Sappho of Lesvos

Born in 612 B.C. on Lesvos, Sappho and her family were exiled to Sicily during her childhood, but she returned to the island to marry and bear a child.

Later, she created a commune of women at ancient Eressos, which promoted the natural bonds of sorority. Her poems — written in a style, Sapphic stanzas, which is named after her — speak of love and tenderness. Her work, along with her social activities, led her to become a torchbearer for homosexual women. Indeed, the word "lesbian" is taken from the island of her birth.

Looks can be deceiving. Nea Moni monastery (Chios) has seen its share of turmoil.

walkways allowing close access to the detail. Greek and Roman statuary, jewelry, and daily utensils are all thoughtfully arranged.

Around the island, Lesvos offers wonderful impressions of Greek village life. Its economy depends far less on tourist earnings and much more on agricultural production (re-established since the problems of the 1920s); therefore, traditional lifestyles are much more common here.

The east of the island has most of the estimated ten million olive trees which produce the island's major crop. They blanket the hills with their silvery leaves, shimmering in the breeze. Small villages with narrow cobbled streets sit among them, built inland to offer protection against pirate raids.

North of Mytilini, stop at the village of **Moria,** where you will find the remains of a huge Roman aqueduct surrounded by grazing goats. **Mandamadhos** village in the far north still carries on a traditional pottery industry on a small scale. On its outskirts, the **Monastery of Taxiarhis** has a revered black icon that is believed to be fashioned from soil wet with the blood of monks slaughtered at the abbey. Continue along this road to reach the pretty coastal town of **Molyvos** (also known by its ancient name, Mithymna), a popular spot for tourists. The medieval streets and Ottoman houses have been transformed into galleries and cafés and a small castle sits proudly above the town. A small harbor below is the place to enjoy lunch.

South of Molyvos, the resort town of **Petra** has an 18th-century townhouse museum and a pretty church built on a large rock at its center. The northwest area offers a complete contrast to the olive groves of the east, with a volcanic landscape totally devoid of trees. The Monastery of Ipsilou sits in this minimalist panorama, reaching up toward the sky as if for inspiration.

Just west of the monastery lies one of the geological wonders of the world. In ancient times, this land had a forest of giant sequoia trees. Volcanic ash covered some of the trees while they were still alive, and over time, their trunks turned to stone. Now known as the Petrified Forest, a number of these trees can be seen, some with every growth ring visible. To the southwest of the **Petrified Forest**, take the road to Eressos and its beach resort of Skala Eressos, birthplace of the poet Sappho.

> **Please**
> *parakaló*

The southern coastline is split by the large inlet of Kolpos Kallonis, but beyond this, in the south of the island, the olive is king, especially around Mount Olimbos, the highest point on Lesvos. Aghiasos village lies in its shadow. A traditional settlement, Aghiasos holds a major festival at its Panagia Vrefokratoussa church on 15 August every year. Plomari on the south coast is a center for fine *ouzo* production, and both Plomari and neighboring Vatara have good beaches, now being developed for tourism. From Lesvos, there are regular summer excursions to the Turkish coastal town of Ayvilik, a base for trips to the sites of ancient Troy and Pergamum.

Chios

On arrival at the port of **Chios Town**, it's tempting to pass through quickly, for it is a dreary welcome to the island. However, Chios island (also known as Hios) has some very beautiful secrets to reveal to those who venture further.

During the 14th century, Chios enjoyed a period of wealth and stability under the Genoese. When the Ottomans took control in 1566, they continued to allow the population privileges unknown on other islands. In part, this related to the gum mastic produced here (a rare and valuable commodity, highly prized for its use in medicine). However, the population of Chios has also experienced very turbulent times, particularly in 1822, when an estimated 20,000 people were massacred by Ottoman forces, following an unsuccessful uprising against Ottoman rule just after the creation of the Greek state in 1821.

Behind its concrete façade (a result of rebuilding after numerous earthquakes), Chios Town has a number of clues to its past. Remnants of a **medieval kastro** and a fine **archaeological museum** housed in a mosque are two of the highlights. There's also the splendid **Argenti Museum and Korai Library** on Odos Korai Street, with its collection of costumes and folk art dating from two thousand years ago.

Out in the countryside, Chios has other attractions to offer. Travel south from Chios Town to reach the mastic groves. Collecting and processing the crop is still a profitable industry. Look out for a number of fine Italian mansions in the plains around **Kambos**. Many still lie in private hands. The twenty mastic villages known collectively as *mastihohoria* were built by the Genoese in the 14–15th centuries. Their intricate and confusing maze of narrow alleyways was deliberately created to confound invaders. They now often do the same to strolling visitors. Most of the villages remain practically unchanged since their creation — save for a plethora of TV antennae — and offer a fascinating view of Greek village life, where tomatoes hang from every window and old folks discuss today's news on their doorsteps.

Pyrgi village, with its walls marked by the incised black and white geometric pattern known as *xysta*, is probably the most visited, although **Mesta** is also beautiful. Following your explorations, head toward the coast and the black pebble beach of **Emborio** to enjoy a cooling dip in the sea.

To the west of Chios Town is a graphic reminder of the bloodbath of 1822. High on a rocky bluff is the village of **Anavatos**, which lost much of its population at the time of the massacre. The women and children of the village chose suicide rather than the Ottoman sword and threw themselves from the rocky precipice at the top of the village. Wander along the empty streets to take in the somber atmosphere.

Nearby is the **Monastery of Nea Moni**, founded in 1049, and one of the most

More Greek greats. A statue of Pythagoras at Pithagorio harbor, Samos.

beautiful Byzantine religious sites in the Aegean. The monastery rests in a fertile valley and is surrounded by plane and pine trees. Mosaics inside a small chapel are of the finest quality and show scenes of the life of Christ. The monastery also suffered damage in 1822. Its more portable treasures were stolen, but a lasting memorial to the massacre is an ossuary, or depository for the bones of the dead. Despite this gruesome reminder, the site is perfect for quiet reflection, and is tended now by a couple of elderly nuns. Beyond Anavatos and Nea Moni are wonderful beaches around the coastal town of **Volissos,** where you will find a quiet place to acquire (or burnish) your suntan.

Samos

A fertile island of vines, olive groves, and pine forest, that

lies just 3 km (2 miles) from the Turkish coast, Samos has taken a back seat in Aegean history since its golden age in the fifth century B.C. Today it is growing in popularity with tourists, and resort facilities are expanding.

The main town **Vathi,** or **Samos Town,** lies on the northeastern coastline in a very sheltered harbor. It has few facilities for tourists, but

Dionysian delights...and you'll find them flourishing in Samos.

a friendly atmosphere and a good **archaeological museum** that exhibits a giant *kouros* 5 m (16 ft) high. Ano Vathi — the older town — sits on the hillside behind and is now bypassed by the new road system.

The much smaller town of **Pithagorio** on the southeastern coast is the site of the ancient capital. It was a center of power in the seventh century B.C. when the Samians were the leading maritime nation on the Aegean. In 538 B.C., power fell into the hands of Polycrates, a ruthless but brilliant leader. He accumulated untold wealth through

Thank you *efheristó*

trade and piracy, funding an extensive construction program and a court which attracted such luminaries as Aesop, the storyteller, and Pythagoras, the mathematician (a local Samian, who later fled the island to escape Polycrates's cruelty). Following the death of Polycrates, Samos was plunged into a sudden and deep decline.

Pithagorio has a very pretty harbor and the ruins of a **Frankish castle**. The only evidence of Polycrates's time is the giant mole which, now strengthened, still stands on the ancient foundations. Two more massive projects can be found in the surrounding countryside. To the west, beyond the airport, are the remains of the **Temple of Hera,** or the Heraion. It would have been the largest temple in the world at the time, but it was never completed. In the hills above Pithagorio is perhaps the most amazing example of Polycrates' wealth and power. He funded the cutting of a tunnel over 1,000 m (3,333 ft) long to bring water to the ancient capital. The **Tunnel of Eupalinos** can be explored but it's not for the claustrophobic.

On the northern coast, the village of **Kokari** has a picturesque harbor, and is a magnet for visitors. Small villages in the interior remain unspoiled, particularly because of their remote and hilly location. Among the prettiest is **Marathokambos,** nestling in the shadow of **Mount Kerkis**. The beaches of Samos provide some of the best conditions for windsurfing in the Aegean, particularly on the western coast. From Samos, it is only a short ferry trip east to the Turkish port of **Kusadasi** and the site of ancient **Ephesus**.

THE NORTHERN AEGEAN

Like Lesvos, Chios, and Samos, the islands of the northern Aegean have been influenced by their proximity to the Turkish coastline, with Limnos in particular playing an important strategic role on shipping lanes to and from the Dardanelles.

The islands also lie close to the northern Greek mainland and the Balkans region, giving their history different influences than that of their neighbors farther south in the Aegean.

Thasos

This small, round tree-covered island is a favorite vacation spot for families from the cities of northern Greece, being only 12 km (8 miles) from the coastline of Macedonia. It has until recently seen fewer foreign visitors, although package flights from Europe now land at the airport of **Kavala** on the mainland for the short ferry crossing.

In ancient times, Thasos was renowned for its sweet white wine, but today its beaches are the major draw. They are considered some of the most beautiful in the Aegean.

The capital, **Thasos Town** or **Limin**, is a modern port built on the site of a medieval fortress and a classical Greek settlement. Large areas of the site have been excavated and the **archaeological museum** houses a comprehensive collection of finds from the site. (As of this writing, the museum is closed for refurbishment, but it is expected to reopen in mid-2000.) There are a number of individual buildings to explore. They include a shrine to Pan built on a rocky outcrop and the **Gate of Parmenon**, reached by way of a steep run of steps — the last remaining ancient port of entry to the town.

Beyond Limin, Thasos is mountainous and covered with pine forest. Tourism has spread throughout the island, but does not overpower its natural charms. The island is famed for its nuts, honey, and fruits, which traditionally have been preserved to last

The past is ever-present in the Greek islands. Here, headless statues in the Temple of Hera.

through the Aegean winters. The closest resort to the capital is **Makriamos**. Hotels and tavernas also line the fine beaches at **Krissi Amoudia** and **Skala Potamias**.

Inland settlements offer fascinating insights into life in bygone ages. **Theologos** was the Ottoman capital of Thasos, and has many preserved mansions. Even higher up in the mountains, **Kastro** was built to evade the attention of marauding pirates, and still proves elusive to all but the most determined visitors.

Limnos

Limnos lies closest to the Dardanelles, and for this reason the island is dominated by the Greek military, which keeps a watchful eye on activity through the straits. It has long been a military station for the dominant nation of the area, and was a major staging point for British and Commonwealth troops before the disastrous Gallipoli campaign of World War I. A cemetery for 900 of these gallant men can be found at **Moudros**, near the harbor where they set forth to their fate.

The capital of the island is **Myrina**. Small stone houses crowd the town center with fine Ottoman houses along the northern edge of town. A small archaeological museum displays finds from the island, including the eastern site of

The Northern Aegean offers some spectacular scenery, such as tranquil Koukounaries Beach, Skiathos.

Polyohni, which was a thriving city before its destruction by earthquake in 2100 B.C. The remains of the Byzantine kastro can also be explored. The coastline north and south of Myrina has some fine stretches of sandy beach, and there is a small resort at Akti Myrina. Unfortunately, poor roads and limited public transportation hinder exploration of other parts of the island.

Samothraki

A series of rocky cliffs line the shoreline of Samothraki which, unlike other islands, has poor natural anchorages. Inland, **Mount Fengari**, the Aegean's highest peak at 1,610 m (5,000 ft), dominates the landscape. It was from here, according to Homer, that the God Poseidon watched the Battle of Troy taking place, looking east across the water. The capital, **Chora Town**, is a classic example of a settlement built out of sight of pirate forces. It nestles in a valley 5 km (3 miles) inland, unseen by passing ships.

Today, the island is little more than a forgotten backwater with few ferry connections to other islands, but its strong natural defenses gave it advantages in ancient times. Until the advent of Christianity, Samothraki was a very important island indeed.

From the late Bronze Age, a center of religious worship developed on the northern coast, which was later dedicated to Castor and Pollux, the patron saints of sailors. It was also home to the powerful Cult of the Underworld. Many, including Philip of Macedon, Alexander the Great's father, traveled here to be initiated into its inner circle.

The remains of the center, the **Sanctuary of the Great Gods** near the town of Paleopoli, now form one of the major archaeological sites in the eastern Aegean. The site ruins, mostly from the Hellenistic period, lie almost overgrown,

but they are perfect for exploring at your own pace.

Highlights include the **Arsinoion rotunda** built for Egyptian Queen Arsinoe in the third century B.C. from marble brought from Thasos. At the time it was the largest circular building in the world, measuring 20 m (65 ft) in diameter. A hill above the theater is where archaeologists found the **Winged Victory of Samothraki**, now in the Louvre in Paris. The more modest museum at the site has many finds, including a fine carved **Temenos** (fourth century B.C.) **frieze** of musicians and dancing girls.

Treasures of the Aegean for sale in Skopelos — the Sporades see plenty of tourists.

Therma on the north coast is still an active spa offering treatments for ailments from rheumatism to infertility. It is also the starting point for three-hour treks to the summit of Mount Fengari, where you can clearly see the Turkish coast — just as Poseidon did.

THE SPORADES

Sporades means scattered, and this group of four islands lies off the Greek mainland in just this fashion. Part of Greece from the moment of statehood, the Sporades islands see many Greek mainland visitors, and were once the exclusive domain of an independent sailing fraternity. Today, a rental fleet makes it possible for almost anyone to enjoy a sail in this dreamy place.

Skiathos

Skiathos is the smallest of the main Sporades islands and lies closest to the Greek mainland. **Skiathos Town**, the only settlement on the island, is a bustling resort, rebuilt after severe damage in World War II. Urbane Athenians spend summer weekends here, rubbing shoulders with the foreign tourists who crowd the bars and clubs. A fleet of rental sailboats uses this port as a base, and commercial ferries ply their regular routes to other islands from here.

The commercial ferry port is separated from the picturesque fishing harbor by **Bourdzi islet,** where you can sit under pine trees and admire the view. The small fort built on the islet now hosts open-air concerts in the summer months. A series of restaurants lines the harborside and the narrow cobbled streets behind. Numerous small boutiques make the old town a good place for souvenir hunting.

However, the lure of Skiathos has always been its beaches — more than 60 along its 44-km (27-mile) coastline. A regular bus service runs along the southern shore, terminating at perhaps the most famous, **Koukounaries Beach**. A long arc of fine sand backed by pine trees, Koukounaries is perhaps the epitome of everything that beach lovers enjoy. Shallow waters, sports, and refreshments add to the fun. Perhaps the only problem is that you will be fighting for sand space with just about every other tourist on the island. A short walk over the hill brings you to **Krassi Beach**, renowned as a nude beach and renamed **Banana Beach** by local people, for obvious reasons!

Beaches along the northern shore are better reached by caique (a small, brightly painted ferry). **Lalaria Beach** is among the most beautiful, with cliffs and natural arches flanking the pebbled bay. The boat trip will also take you past **Kastro**, the long abandoned 16th-century capital. Now in ruins, it sits atop a rocky promontory.

Skopelos

The population of Skopelos is renowned for its friendliness and hospitality, and the natural beauty of the island is equally inviting. **Skopelos Town** is one of the most impressive towns of its size in the Aegean, in part because it is also among the most original — little damaged either by war or earthquakes. Its gray-tiled roofs cascade down an amphitheater-shaped hill toward the tiny port. Round church towers topped with tiny crosses punctuate the skyline. The ruined **Venetian castle** atop a small hill offers panoramic views over the whole town, while the roof of the particularly beautiful **Church of Christ** along the harbor stands out from the open sea.

The interior of the island is a wonderful mixture of mountainous dark pine forest and farmland. There are fewer beaches than on other islands in the Sporades, but yachts moor in the numerous rocky inlets around the coastline where there is excellent snorkeling and swimming. **Panormos** and **Agnondas** on the south coast attract tourists, as does **Stafylos Beach,** where the tomb of an ancient king of the same name was found in 1927.

Alonissos

Alonissos has been settled longer than any other Aegean island, estimated by archaeologists to date from 100,000 B.C., and was valued by many leaders in classical Greek times. Yet, in this century, the island has suffered a number of severe setbacks that, until recently, made it a backwater of the Aegean. The wine produced on the island was prized for many centuries, but a bout of Phylloxera disease killed the vines, and a large earthquake in 1965 destroyed the island's major settlement.

Today, people visit Alonissos for its natural beauty. Much of the sea around the island has been designated as a marine conservation area called the **Sporades Marine Park**, which includes several small islands offshore. This protects a population of monk seals and other marine life, as well as archaeological remains on the seabed.

Palea Alonissos, destroyed in the earthquake, is a five-minute bus ride inland from the port of **Patitiri**, and its old houses are slowly being revived with outside investment. Views from its Byzantine walls are spectacular. The road network is limited, but there is a bus service to the

Divine inspiration...An aesthetic treat in its own right, the
Church of Christ also offers great views of Skopelos Harbor.

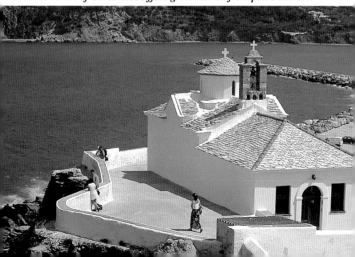

Kokkinokastro Peninsula where the most popular beaches lie. Fleets of small caiques travel to more remote beaches that lie all around the coastline.

Skyros

The largest and most remote island in the Sporades — a two-hour ferry journey southeast of Skiathos — Skyros has been little affected by tourism. It is a mountainous island and its inhabitants have a rugged individuality that matches the landscape. The whole island takes part in the **Skyros Carnival**, an annual event that takes place in the days leading up to Lent. Grotesque animal costumes are worn, bawdy jokes are exchanged, and ritual dances are performed.

The main settlement, **Skyros Town** on the east coast, is topped with a **Byzantine/Venetian kastro**. Legend says that Theseus was thrown to his death here, many generations ago. In the north of the town, a local artist, Manos Faltaïts, has developed a museum of Skyrian folklore and tradition. The **Faltaïts Museum** is housed in an old mansion and features costumes, arts and crafts, and photographs. There is also an archaeological museum that displays older relics, including examples of Mycenaean pottery. To the north is the long, sandy **Magazia Beach.**

The south of the island is mountainous and barren and traveling there is difficult. British poet **Rupert Brooke** is buried at **Tris Boukes**, a bay in the far south. He died in 1915 while on his way to fight in the Dardanelles during World War I.

To the north, wooded hillsides and olive groves surround the airport. Ferries arrive at Linaria on the east coast, and in pastures around the village it is possible to see the last examples of the famed **Skyrian miniature horses**. This species, about the same size as Shetland ponies and found only here, is descended from the ancient Pikermic breed.

WHAT TO DO

Island life is certainly relaxing, and in the Aegean there is no pressure on you to do anything except read that novel you always promised yourself that you would. However, for those with the energy, there's plenty to do.

Beaches

Beaches come in all sizes, from the tiny cove where you can spend the day alone, to wide sandy bays where you can be sure of the company of hundreds. Some have ample shade and others are treeless, catering to ardent sun worshippers. Many people decry the pebble beach, preferring soft sand; however, in the summer Meltemi winds, pebbles of coin size don't blow around and spoil your day, whereas sand does. Santorini has volcanic sand in a choice of black or red. It absorbs heat much more efficiently than yellow sand and therefore becomes much hotter in the heat of the day — not good for small children who want to run around and play. For fine sand beaches, you will find some of the best are Koukanaries on Skiathos, Golden on Paros, and Paradise on Mykonos. There's also Milopotamos on Ios, and Makriamos on Thasos.

In Europe in the 1960s, the Greek islands became renowned for their laid-back attitude toward visitors. Naturists flocked to the area. Although things have changed a little today, there are still nude beaches on some of the islands, notably Paradise and Super-Paradise on Mykonos and Banana Beach on Skiathos. However, on most islands, nudity is not official policy and Greek family beaches will certainly not be clothing-optional. If you want to be sure of not catching sight of anything risqué, follow the local people.

SPORTS

You'll find a wide range of water sports available in the islands. Jetskiing is popular almost everywhere, with half-hour rentals common. Windsurfing is best where the prevailing winds and wide sandy bays allow the sail to catch the breeze. Conditions are particularly strong on the west coast of Paros, where the World Windsurfing Championships are held every year. You can also find good offshore conditions at Naxos, Samos, and Kos.

Many beaches also have water rides in which you sit on or in a rubber shape and are pulled along behind a speed boat. Great fun for kids, but unnerving for watching parents.

Diving

Although the warm, clear waters of the Aegean constitute a near-perfect diving environment, until recently the Greek

All smiles from this Santorini scuba team! And it's easy to guess why — diving conditions are optimal in the Aegean.

government was rightly concerned about the possible damage divers might do to submerged ancient sites, and diving was prohibited. However, attitudes have changed, and diving is now a legal and welcomed activity, provided you dive with an approved and registered organization. A number of companies are already operating on islands around the Aegean. They supervise dives and provide transport to the sites, usually two sessions a day in high season.

Each dive center is registered by the Greek government, and qualified to offer training for novice divers and supervision for qualified divers. All centers are affiliated with one of the major certifying bodies, with PADI (Professional Association of Diving Instructors) being the most common. The basic qualification, the Open Water certificate, takes five days to complete. On completion, you will be allowed to dive with an instructor to a depth of 18 m (60 ft). This enables you to experience many dive sites in the Aegean Sea.

Many centers also offer an introductory session commonly known as the Discover Scuba program. This involves a morning or afternoon of theory and shallow-water work, giving you an opportunity to try out the basic techniques before committing yourself a full open-water course.

Mykonos has had a head start as far as diving is concerned because it was never banned here (no ancient sites to protect). Dive Adventures at Paradise Beach (Tel. 02890 26539 in season; Tel. 010 7560552 during the winter) is an established center. Santorini also has interesting dive sites. You can discover the sheer underwater walls in the caldera, or visit the reef off the eastern coast. Contact Mediterranean Dive Club at Perissa Beach (Tel. 02860 83080 in season; Tel. 010 4125376 during the winter).

Paros has cave, reef, and wreck diving around its shores, giving the diver a wide range of environments to explore.

Several dive centers operate on the island, including Santa Maria Diving Club at Naoussa on the northern coast (Tel. 02840 385307; fax 02840 53007). Kos has some well-organised dive operators at its resorts. Contact Theokritos Travel 300 m (984 ft) from the beach on the main road in Tigaki (Tel. 02420 69666; fax 02420 69112).

Sailing

With its centuries-old seafaring tradition, the Aegean has long been a lure to sports sailors. Many of the elite of Athens have sailed the short distance from the capital for a weekend at a deserted inlet. Until recently, there was little for ordinary mortals who lacked a yacht, but now there are sailing fleets waiting to be hired either bare (for qualified sailors) or with a crew to do the work for you. Flotillas can be organized for gregarious island-hopping or you can wend your own way at your own pace. The largest hire fleets are found in Athens, Skiathos, or on Kos. Contact Sunsail, a UK-based company (Tel. 44 (0)1705 222222; fax 44 (0)1705 219827; web site <www.sunsail.com>) for further details.

Snorkeling

You can rent or buy snorkeling equipment in all the major resorts, allowing you to explore the beach shallows and hundreds of rocky inlets that can be found on most islands. You'll see sea urchins, shoals of fish, and even small octopuses that make their homes in rocky crevices just off shore.

Walking and Hiking

Exploring the coastline or interior of the Greek islands offers a different experience with each season of year. In late spring, the hillsides are awash with flowers, and crops such as corn give the fields a golden hue. As summer progresses and the crops are harvested (usually early July), the ground dries and becomes dustier. The distinctive sound of the cicada chirps through the heat of the day. In autumn, the earth gives back the heat it absorbed during the summer, as the air begins to cool. Spring and autumn offer the clearest air for panoramic views of the surrounding land; in summer, a heat-induced haze rises, cutting long distance visibility.

Easy riders — rent a motorcycle or scooter and see the islands at your own speed.

There are some interesting, though not too difficult hikes on various islands. Don't forget to take a supply of water and wear sturdy footwear. If you walk in summer, early morning or late afternoon is best.

On Santorini, there is a footpath along the lip of the caldera which leads from the town of Fira to Oia, offering stunning views of the whole area. On Paros, the marble-clad Byzantine road at Lefkes takes you down the valley to Karampoli. There are hundreds of old donkey trails to explore on Tinos. On Karpathos, you can walk from the traditional settlement of Olimbos to the shrine of St. John in the north of the island.

On Samothraki, you can climb to the summit of Mount Fengari, where the God Poseidon watched the Trojan War reach its tragic climax. On Naxos, you can walk through the pretty villages of the Tragea Valley and the foothills of Mount Zas, admiring Byzantine churches and exploring olive groves at your leisure.

SHOPPING

The weaving maze of small streets that comprise many old towns in the Aegean contains a fascinating mixture of art and sculpture galleries, jewelers, clothing boutiques, and stores selling collectibles. It's possible to spend hours browsing for the perfect souvenir.

Antiques

For serious collectors, there are genuine antiques for sale throughout the Aegean (anything made or produced before 1821 is officially classified as an antique). These could be in the form of sculpture, pottery, or icons. They will require proper accreditation, and in some cases a permit, if they are to be exported from the country. The antiques dealer should be able to advise you in this process.

Open *aniktós*
Closed *klistós*

For those whose budget or expertise won't stretch to the real thing, reproductions of these same articles are sold. Quality and prices vary.

Art and Sculpture

One thing you'll immediately notice is that prices for articles that are based on the same design and may, at first glance, look the same, range from only a few dollars to many thousands of dollars. This is because there is tremendous variation in the quality of the materials used and the skills of the workmen involved. You will soon be able to discern this after visiting a few stores and closely examining the products. Look out for the weight of a piece of pottery or sculpture and the amount of detail in the decoration or the carving.

Popular traditional themes are Cycladic figures (especially on the Cyclades islands) or pottery with scenes taken from ancient Greek frescoes or mosaics. At the bottom end of the market, try refrigerator magnets in the shape of Ionian or Corinthian columns!

Modern artists flock to the main islands, both to work and to sell their pieces. Often a traditional house will be transformed

---

The Genuine Icon

Icon is the word used to describe a religious portrait, usually of a saint or apostle. Icons developed from the two-dimensional *fayum* paintings that covered the faces of the dead in the sarcophagi of Egyptian mummies. They lie at the heart of Byzantine or Orthodox worship and form a focus for prayer. Some icons are said to possess miraculous healing powers or the ability to perform miracles; although in a church, all are considered holy. The characteristic gold leaf used in their production symbolizes the glory of God. The earliest examples date from the later part of the first millennium.

Icon painters created works for churches but also for private clients. For centuries, they were popular souvenirs of the grand European Tour or religious pilgrimage. However, modern production methods, including thin artificial canvas and gaudy synthetic colors, saw them lose favor.

In recent years, there has been a rebirth in icon painting using traditional methods, both for church renovations and for commercial sale. Natural pigments and egg tempura (egg yolk and vinegar) binding are painstakingly mixed and applied to a canvas bound over wood. The gold leaf is then applied and the whole image is given a patina. This time-consuming work is exquisite and correspondingly expensive.

into a small and enticing gallery. The range of styles and media means that you are sure to find a unique souvenir that suites your taste.

Clothing

Traditional Greek clothing is little in evidence, but most of the islands have narrow lanes festooned with cool cotton or cheesecloth pants, tops, and dresses, all of which are ideal for the summer climate. You will also find the ubiquitous T-shirt in a variety of styles, along with swimwear and footwear. In fact, you may not even need to pack any clothes for your trip. Just buy them when you arrive!

Pottery featuring classical Greek motifs make for memorable souvenirs.

Santorini and Mykonos in particular have a plethora of designer clothing and shoes from Europe and the United States. Many of the familiar names (Armani, DNKY) have their own air-conditioned boutiques. Traditional thick cotton sweaters can still be found on Mykonos (ideal for evening in the late season), although outlets are rapidly closing to make way for contemporary boutiques. Buy soon or you may miss the chance.

Food

The abundant fruit grown on the islands in the summer continues to be preserved to last through the cold winters. Cherries, plums, figs, and other fruits are made into jams.

Bees harvest the pollen of the wild herbs on the hillsides to produce delicious honey to which fresh nuts (almonds or walnuts) are added. Olives are preserved either in oil or brine, or simply take home a bottle of extra virgin olive oil both for cooking and to make delicious salad dressings.

Jewelry

Precious stones glitter in shops on the streets of Mykonos and Santorini, and you can choose as many carats as your budget can handle. Gold and silver are sold by weight, with relatively little extra cost added for workmanship, making them a good buy. Ancient Greek designs are very much in evidence in gold, silver, and non-precious metals. Favorite designs are Hellenic, Minoan, and Macedonian.

> The evening stroll, or *volta*, has its own complicated rules. Never rush, the idea is to be seen; and never overtake the senior members of the community (this is considered disrespectful).

At the other extreme, there are many forms of hippie jewelry from anklets in metal or leather and navel studs, to finger and toe rings.

Leather Wares

Greek islanders have always worked the leather from their arable herds to make handbags, purses, belts, and footwear in a variety of styles and patterns, although it cannot match the quality of the Italian-produced leather products sold in boutiques in Santorini and Mykonos. However, prices for native-produced items are cheaper.

ENTERTAINMENT

Nightlife varies from island to island, and on some of the smaller islands, an evening will revolve around dinner and conversation at the local taverna, or a stroll along the seafront. However, traditional Greek dances and musical performances, as well as clubs with DJs spinning dance music can be found.

Music and Dance

For many, the image of Greek music and dance is inexorably linked to the film *Zorba the Greek*. Anthony Quinn performs the *syrtaki* dance (in fact, an amalgam of several different traditional dances) to the sound of the bouzouki, a stringed-guitar instrument that produces melodic, slightly metallic sounds. When played live, it has a haunting melody but taverna owners do have the irritating habit of playing it at high decibels through overloaded speakers.

This does a great disservice to the Greek musical tradition, which is rich and varied and goes back hundreds of years. Musical rhythms were traditionally matched to the complex cadences of the epic poetry of Greece. Because these rhythms differ from the four beats to a bar notation we are accustomed

To Buy or Not to Buy

Whichever island you choose for your Aegean odyssey, chances are it has its own souvenir specialty. Here are some of the outstanding handicrafts or natural products of the islands:

Kalymnos	Sponges
Karpathos	Embroidery, lace, and crochet work
Lesvos	Olive oil and ouzo
Mykonos	Thick cotton sweaters
Naxos	Kitron, a lemon liqueur
Sifnos	Fine pottery decorated with classical themes
Thasos	Pine honey and fruit preserves
Tinos	Marble from Pyrgos, incense, offertory and votive candles

to in the West, Greek music sometimes can be difficult to follow.

Each region of Greece has its own particular songs and dances. The music of the southern islands has a traditional style called *nisiotika*, while in the northern Aegean, a style called *sandouri* prevails. Most islands have a *syrtos* dance, or steps performed in the round.

In the 1920s, the tempestuous time of Turkish liberation, these dances instantly became known as the classical styles. Also at that time, a new style, *rembetiko*, was created. Many Greeks in

Opa! The Greeks know how to put on a dance performance. Catch one if you can.

Asia Minor were forced to leave their homes and brought an influence of eastern cadences with them. The themes found in rembetiko are those closest to the hearts of the common man: lost love, poverty, social division, and discrimination. It's no surprise to discover that it is the most popular form of Greek music heard on the radio today.

It is becoming more difficult to see performances on the islands. Cultural festivals are one opportunity, but the better way is at a private wedding or feast day when the performances are set in their true context. Many islands will also have one venue for Greek night, an evening of culinary and cultural delights. While Greek night may strike some visitors as contrived, it is nonetheless an opportunity to see a local art form.

Ancient Greek Drama

Performances of classical Greek theater are found on some islands. Although it is now performed in the modern rather than the classical Greek language, it is still not easy to understand, so try to find an English copy of the plot before the performance begins. When you see the plays performed in the ancient theaters of classical or Roman times, such as those on Thasos or Kos, it makes it all worthwhile. Sitting in the balmy evening air with only natural acoustics to aid the actor's delivery is a special experience.

Clubbing

For those who can't go on vacation without the hope of dancing to throbbing music well into the early hours of the morning, look no further than the towns of Fira on Santorini, Mykonos Town on Mykonos, Skiathos Town on Skiathos, or Chora on Ios. Here you can party to your heart's content.

ACTIVITIES FOR CHILDREN

Children are welcomed all over the Greek islands, and they will be fussed over and indulged in cafés and restaurants. Young children love beach activities, and as the Aegean has little tidal range and many wide shallow bays, it has many places which are safe for paddling and swimming. Sandy beaches are more fun than pebbles for castle building and hole digging, so bear that in mind when choosing your island. Do remember that if you are taking young children to the beach the sun can be extremely hot. Keep young skins safe by covering them with sunblock or a T-shirt, even when in the water.

For older children, the range of water sports found in the popular resorts offers an exciting challenge. From pedal boats and canoes to windsurfing and jetskiing, the choice is yours. For even more fun, try the water park Kolymithres on Paros — hours of fun for all ages.

Shopping is another possibility. Even the most meager allowance will fund a shopping spree in the narrow streets of the Greek island towns. Small, cheap souvenirs are readily available in the forms of pottery, sculpture, jewelry, and clothing.

A Crusader castle brings swashbuckling to life, so try a trip to the walls of Mytilini or Kos Castle to become a knight of yore. Caique trips also are popular. These small, prettily painted boats ply their routes from main towns to nearby beaches. Children love to watch the coastline go by, or point out shoals of small fish swimming in the clear water. Yet another fun, if offbeat, idea is to ride a donkey from the port up to Fira town on Santorini. Finally, visit the village of Olimbos on Karpathos, where the people, including children, wear elaborate and beautiful traditional costumes.

Water babies...With its temperate water, sandy beaches, and shallow coves, the islands are a kids' playground.

Calendar of Events

There are over 300 Saints' Days celebrated in the islands each year. Listed below are the "larger" events and national celebrations shared with the Greek mainland.

1 January: Called Protochronia, but also St. Basil's Day. When sprigs of basil are given as traditional gifts.

6 January: Epiphany, when young men dive into the cold waters to recover a crucifix. Those who do are considered blessed for the year.

February/March: Carnival time on many islands, particularly Skyros, Chios, Paros, and Karpathos.

26 March: Greek Independence Day, military parades.

Clean Monday: First day of Orthodox Lent, marked by frugal meals. House cleaning and laundry also are undertaken with enthusiasm on this day.

Easter: Easter is the most important of the Orthodox holidays. Candlelit processions follow a flower-decked bier on Good Friday. On Holy Saturday, a sacred flame is passed to each household to light a lamp of faith. On Sunday, lambs are sacrificed and roasted, signifying the commencement of another spring.

23 April: St. George's Day, a feast celebrating Greece's patron saint, with horse races and dancing on Limnos and Kos.

1 May: May Day, marked by processions and flower festivals.

May: Ceremony for sponge fishermen on Kalymnos, as they head out to sea.

May/June: Bull ceremonies on Lesvos.

15 August: Assumption Day, celebrated with processions on Tinos and Lesvos, and a festival on Paros.

August: Drama festival on Thasos; Hippocratia festival on Kos.

28 October: National *Ochi* ("No") Day, commemorating Greek defiance of the Italian invasion of 1940.

December: Caroling in the days before Christmas and on New Year's Eve.

EATING OUT

Greek cuisine makes no pretense of emulating the classic cuisine of countries like France, however it has always used local and often seasonal ingredients at their peak of flavor and freshness. The people have relied on staples such as olive oil, wild herbs, seafood, lamb, or goat meat and an abundance of fresh vegetables, fruit, and nuts since the islands were settled several millennia ago. Today, the Greek diet is considered one of the healthiest in the world, and its population is among the longest living. The extensive use of vegetables makes eating out a delight for vegetarians.

Over the centuries, the various cultures that have ruled the islands have left behind their own influences, which can still be experienced today. The Venetians and the Genoese, for example, left a legacy of tomato sauce that is used in many contemporary dishes; the Ottomans contributed yogurt, souvlaki (kebabs), and wonderfully strong dark coffee.

Where to Eat

The Greek islands have a fascinating range of eateries that, at first glance, can be a little confusing for the visitor. However, once you realize that, traditionally, Greek families never ate a three-course meal in one establishment, it brings the whole picture together. The appetizer and main course are eaten first, then one moves on to another place for sweets, and yet another for coffee. As tourist numbers grow, this system is breaking down on many islands and changing to the European or American custom of eating an entire meal in the same restaurant. However, on islands where traditions are strong, you will still find the following places to eat:

The *ouzerie* is a traditional establishment selling not only the fiery but pleasant alcoholic drink, *ouzo,* but also the *mezedes* dishes which accompany it. Ouzo is never drunk on an empty stomach. The mezedes dishes can simply be a couple of appetizers or a full meal of several different small dishes. All will be absolutely fresh and delicious. Many ouzeries have octopuses hanging out to dry and tenderize. Octopus or squid is traditionally served with ouzo, but it is not compulsory. You will also have a range of hot and cold vegetable and meat dishes to choose from.

Visit the *psistaria* (the *gyro* and *souvlaki* shop). These most ancient of fast foods make tasty lunches or snacks. Later, peruse the amazing choices at the *zacharoplastia* (pastry shop) or the *galaktopolio*, which specializes in yogurt, cheese, and other dairy dishes.

The *kafeneion* is the Greek coffee shop, traditionally the domain of the male, and it is still so in the inland villages on

With its mouth-watering, slow-roasted lamb and beef barbecues, Greece is a carnivore's delight.

islands such as Chios and Lesvos. Usually very plainly decorated, with a few old tables and chairs outside, it is a place
of heated political debates and serious backgammon games.

However, the *taverna* (you'll find it spelled *tabepna* on many
Greek signs because b is pronounced v and p is pronounced
r in the Greek language) is at
the heart of Greek hospitality.
It's where the appetizer and
entrée courses have always
been taken.

In the last few years,
there has been a great move
to cash in on the increase in
the number of visitors and
pass off frozen or mass-
produced food as traditional home-cooked dishes. To

> **You may be offered a sweet
> course in a *taverna,* only to
> see your waiter go rushing
> off around the corner to
> return with your choice. In
> deference to a visitor's desire
> to have a full meal at one
> establishment, he has rushed
> to the local *zacharoplastia* or
> *galaktopolio* to purchase a
> portion for you. The cost will
> be added to your bill.**

find authentic cuisine, follow the local people. You may
find yourself in some back street eatery away from the
pretty views, but you can be sure that the food is excellent.

When to Eat

Many tavernas in the major resorts will be open to serve
breakfast, lunch, and dinner (breakfast includes a cooked
English breakfast). However, traditionally, breakfast has
been a small meal for Greeks (basically, a continental breakfast of bread, jam or honey, and coffee.) Lunch is taken
around 3pm, followed by a siesta before work begins again
around 5:30pm. Dinner is taken late, usually around 10pm,
though in summer tavernas will serve food as late as 1am.

Conversely, if you want to eat early, most tavernas will
begin their evening service at around 6pm. You will definitely have your choice of table if you eat before 7:30pm, but

restaurants will lack the colorful atmosphere of the later evening when local people come out to eat.

The Menu

In most traditional restaurants, you will be presented with an extensive menu list but not everything on it is available. Many foods are seasonal or made in batches (such as *moussaka*). Items currently available will have a price in pencil beside them.

Some of the best and most authentic restaurants will not even have a menu. The cook will prepare whatever is in season, and only a couple of dishes, to ensure that they are perfect. You simply go into the kitchen to see what looks and smells most enticing, then make your choice.

If the taverna has a barbecue, you will be invited to the grill to make your choice or to the ice table to choose your seafood. This is sold by weight, so always ask how much it will be before it is cooked to avoid a nasty surprise later.

> Service is relaxed in Greek tavernas. Greeks view eating as a social occasion, not just a method of taking in calories. They're happy to sit and chat between courses and watch the world go by.

All restaurants will render a cover charge. This includes a serving of bread and is usually no more than €1 per person.

Appetizers

Greece is one country where appetizers can constitute a full meal. *Mezedes* (a selection of small appetizer dishes), shared by the whole table, is a fun and relaxing way to eat. You simply have as little or as much as you want and keep ordering until you have had your fill. As many are meatless, they are perfect for vegetarians, and waiters have no qualms about taking orders for an "appetizers-only" meal.

The most popular mezedes are *tzatziki*, a yogurt dip flavored with garlic, cucumber, and mint; *dolmades*, vine leaves stuffed with rice and vegetables, which can be served hot or cold; and olives. There's *tarama*, cod-roe paste blended with breadcrumbs, olive oil, and lemon juice; *fasolya,* large beans in tomato sauce; and also *kalamarakia tiganita*, small pieces of deep-fried squid. *Tiropitikia*, small pastry parcels filled with cheese, is also common, along with *pastourma,* a kind of garlic sausage made with mutton or beef, and *keftedes*, small

A classic Greek salad makes for a delicious appetizer — or a meal in itself.

meatballs flavored with coriander and spices. The strangely oriental-sounding *saganaki* is a slice of cheese coated in breadcrumbs and then fried.

Greek salad or *horiatika* (literally translated as "village salad") is tomato, cucumber, onion, and olives topped with feta cheese, and can be taken as a meal in itself. When adding salad dressing (bottles of olive oil and wine vinegar are found with other condiments on the table), always add vinegar to the salad first, followed by oil. This is done to taste, though your salad may arrive already dressed.

Soups are staples of the Greek diet in winter, but their availability is more limited in summer. Fish soup is a standard on many menus. *Avgolemono*, a chicken broth with egg, lemon, and rice, is delicious, but less commonly found. An Easter soup is *magaritsa*, made with lamb tripe, egg, lemon, and lettuce. Traditionally, it is eaten to break the Lenten fast. *Revythia soupa* is a thick, chick-pea offering especially enjoyed on Sifnos.

Fish

With all the pretty harbors full of boats in the Aegean, it's no surprise that seafood forms a major part of the diet for islanders. You will find the day's catch on ice outside a taverna. The waiter will ask you to make your choice, which will be weighed and priced before cooking. Seafood is always a relatively expensive option by Greek standards, because of over-fishing in the surrounding seas. The most common fish are *barbounia* (red mullet), *xifias* (swordfish), and *lithrini* (bream). Seafood is always best served simply, and it is often grilled with fresh lemon. *Marides* (little fish or whitebait) is served fried, but you can find seafood served with white wine sauce, or sauces mixed with feta cheese.

> **Cheers! (when drinking) yámas!**

Meat

Wherever you look, you will see barbecued meats. Fast foods include *gyros* (thin slices of meat cut from a spit and served with salad on pita bread) or *souvlaki* (small chunks of meat on a skewer, also known by the Turkish name *kebab*). More formal barbecued dishes may include whole chickens, sides of lamb and veal, or stuffed loin of pork, all cooked to a melting perfection. *Brizole* is a basic steak, but it may automatically come *bien cuit* (rare)*, rather than *à point* (well done)*. Roasted or barbecued lamb is the traditional Easter fare.

These dishes are easy to identify and order, but there are many superb slow-cooked oven dishes and stews, which are well worth trying. *Kleftiko* is braised lamb with tomatoes, while *stifado* is braised beef with onions. Each comes in a small earthenware pot that keeps the contents piping hot.

Greece's most famous dish is probably *moussaka*, successive layers of eggplant (aubergine) and minced lamb with onions topped with béchamel sauce. At its best, it should be firm but succulent and aromatic with herbs. The best restaurants will make a fresh batch daily. Once it is gone, you'll have to wait until tomorrow. *Pastitsio* is another layered dish, this time of pasta (macaroni), meat, and tomato sauce. It is a dish that comes straight from the Italian period in the history of the Aegean.

The northern islands have *kouneli* (rabbit) and *perdikes* (partridge), both caught by hunters and traditionally served sautéed. For those who want a hot meatless dish, there's *yemitsa*, tomatoes, eggplants, or bell peppers stuffed with a delicious rice and vegetable mixture.

Dessert

Most tavernas will bring a plate of fresh fruit as a finale to your meal. Often it is melon, or perhaps fresh figs. If you feel the need for something more substantial, a taverna will rarely have a full selection of desserts. The zacharoplastia is the place to go. Here you will find *baklava* (honey-soaked flaky pastry with walnuts), *katiafi* (shredded wheat filled with chopped almonds and honey), or *pita me meli* (honey cake). If you prefer dairy desserts, try delicious Greek yogurt with honey or fruit or *galaktobouriki* (custard pie).

Drinks

Dionysos, the God of Wine, made his home on Naxos, but in classical times, many more Greek islands produced wine. For many centuries it was a major industry. Today, though the vintages aren't of French quality, there are some excel-

*Ouzo, ouzo, and more ouzo...
Indulge yourself, but watch
out — it packs a punch!*

lent producers and a good range to choose from. You will also find that a number of wines produced on the Greek mainland are also imported to the islands.

Another option is to order wine from the barrel. This basic village wine will be served young and cool. Greece also produces a wine flavored with resin called *retsina* (particularly useful in ancient times, because it kept the wine fresh in the hot climate). Retsina goes well with the Greek diet and the hot climate, but it is an acquired taste.

Ouzo is another drink that suits the hot climate. Taken as an aperitif, neat, or with ice and water, the aniseed flavor seems to cool the blood. However, don't overdo it as too much can pack a mighty hangover!

Those who prefer beer can find Amstel and Heineken brewed under license on the Greek mainland. Mythos is a native Hellenic beer which has a very crisp taste.

Non-Alcoholic Drinks

Greece has fallen in love with the *café frappe* (strong cold coffee served over ice). It's especially refreshing in the heat of the day. Hot coffee is made *ellenikos* or Greek style (indistinguishable from Turkish coffee). It's always freshly brewed in individual copper pots and served in small cups. It will automatically arrive *glykivastro* (very sweet) unless you order *metrio* (medium) or *sketo* (without sugar). Those who prefer instant coffee can order a drink known simply by its trade name, Nescafé or *nes*.

To Help You Order...

The following words and phrases should help you when ordering food and drink. You may want to purchase a copy of the *Berlitz European Menu Reader* or the *Berlitz Greek Phrase Book and Dictionary*. Both have a comprehensive glossary of Greek wining and dining.

I'd like a/an/some…	**Tha íthela…**
Could we have a table?	**Tha boroúsame na échoume éna trapézi?**

napkin	**trapezo-mándillo**	honey	**méli**
cutlery	**machero-pírouna**	water	**neró**
glass	**potíri**	egg	**avgó**
one	**éna/mia**	beef	**vodinó**
two	**dhío**	pork	**kirinó**
three	**tris/tría**	chicken	**kotópoulo**
four	**tésera**	prawns	**garída**
bread	**psomí**	octopus	**ktapódi**
wine	**krasí**	eggplant	**melitsána**
beer	**bíra**	(aubergine)	
fish	**psarí**	garlic	**skórdo**
fruit	**froúta**	ice cream	**pagotó**
meat	**kréas**	olives	**elyés**
milk	**gála**	lamb	**arní**
sugar	**záchari**	roasted or grilled	**psitó**
salt	**aláti**	butter	**vútiro**
pepper	**pipéri**	chick peas	**revíthya**

HANDY TRAVEL TIPS

An A–Z Summary of Practical Information

A Accommodation 103
Airports 104
Antiquities 105
B Bicycle and Motor
Scooter Rental 105
Budgeting for Your
Trip 106
C Camping 107
Car Rental/Hire 107
Climate 108
Clothing 108
Complaints 109
Crime and Safety 109
Customs and Entry
Requirements 110
D Driving 111
E Electricity 114
Embassies and
Consulates 114
Emergencies 114
G Gay and Lesbian
Travelers 115
Getting There 115

Guides and Tours 117
H Health and Medical
Care 118
Holidays 119
L Language 120
M Maps 121
Media 121
Money 122
O Opening Hours 123
P Police 123
Post Offices 124
Public
Transportation 124
R Religion 124
T Telephone 124
Time Zones 125
Tipping 125
Toilets 125
Tourist
Information 125
W Web Sites 127
Weights and
Measures 127
Y Youth Hostels 127

A

ACCOMMODATION (See CAMPING, YOUTH HOSTELS, and the list of Recommended Hotels starting on page 128)
Hotels are divided into six classes: Luxury, A, B, C, D, and E. Room rates for all categories except luxury are set by the Greek government. The classes are dictated by the facilities at the hotel, not the quality of the rooms. This means that a class C hotel room may be just as acceptable as a class A hotel room, but the hotel will not have facilities such as a conference room. Most hotels in class C and above are clean and reasonably furnished.

There are many lower-rated hotels, and relatively few in the higher rating categories. On the more popular islands such as Mykonos, Santorini, Skiathos, or Kos, it is imperative to book in advance.

Most double rooms in Greece come with two single beds. If you wish to have a queen-size bed instead, be sure to specify a "matrimonial" bed when you make your booking. Most hotels only have one or two rooms with queen-size beds.

If you travel in peak season, there may be a surcharge if you book for less than three days. Local and national taxes (around 4% and 8% respectively, plus a service charge of around 12%) will added to the posted price.

If you need advice, the Greek National Tourist Office (GNTO) can help with bookings and reservations. (Note that signs for GNTO offices in the islands read "EOT.")

The GNTO (see TOURIST INFORMATION) has an information booklet on each island group that lists all hotels in the upper categories on the back page, with telephone numbers.

Private Accommodation Many families rent out rooms or studios to visitors. If you arrive without a reservation, consider this kind of accommodation, particularly in peak season. If you arrive by ferry, there will be someone at the port with photographs to show you his accommodation. It helps to know the geography of the island, as some private accommodation are some distance away from the main towns or resorts. Maintain a skeptical attitude toward any distances mentioned, and have a map ready so that the owner can point out exactly where his property is.

Villas For families or others who want to stay on one island for some time, renting a house or villa can be both cost-effective and a great way to see the island somewhat as the locals do. Villas can be rented for a week or more, although some owners stipulate one month at a minimum. Always check exactly what facilities are provided. Most come with towels, bed linens, and full kitchen facilities; some have pools and vehicles included in the rental. Tour operators and travel agents in your home country can assist you with bookings. Otherwise, contact the local office of the GNTO (see page 126).

AIRPORTS (see also GETTING THERE)

Most internationally scheduled flights land at the new Eleftherinos Venizolos International Airport, which was completed in 2001. The site of the old Athens Hellenikon International Airport is being developed as a public park and for facilities for the 2004 Olympic Games. The airport acts as a hub for domestic flights to the islands. If you're heading into Athens, however, bear in mind that the new airport is some way out of the city in Spata. The most convenient way to get to the center is on the E95 bus that runs to and from Syntagma Square (from where you can take the metro to elsewhere in the city).

If you want to travel direct from the airport to the port of Piraeus for onward ferry journeys, you can either go through the city or take another bus, the E96. Taxis from the airport are expensive, so the bus is probably the best option for most people. If you do take a taxi, always insist that your driver turn on his meter at the start of your journey.

For the northern Aegean Islands (Thassos, Limnos, and Samothraki), it is possible to fly directly to Thessaloniki on the northern Greek mainland for ferry connections or onward flights.

The following islands have airports with domestic service: Astypalea, Karpathos, Kastellorizo, Kos, Limnos, Milos, Mykonos, Lesvos (Mytilini), Naxos, Paros, Samos, Santorini (Thira), Skiathos, Skyros, and Syros.

Many British and Irish package tour companies fly directly to some of the Greek Islands. Kos, Skiathos, Lesvos, and Mykonos are the main airports used.

ANTIQUITIES

The Greek authorities are very concerned about the loss of antiquities and other national treasures. If you intend to buy an old piece, be it an icon or a piece of statuary, always deal with a reputable dealer and keep your receipts. Genuine antiquities need a permit. Exporting antiquities without a permit is a serious offense.

B

BICYCLE AND MOTOR SCOOTER RENTAL

Bicycles Many islands and resorts are ideal places to rent bicycles, though some islands are too hilly to make it a viable way to tour around. For those who want to cycle around town or to the beach it is an ideal form of transport, however. Ordinary bicycles can be rented in most major resorts for around €6 per day.

Motor Scooters Motor scooters or mopeds are very popular, and they can be one of the best ways to get around all but the largest Greek islands. Rental is relatively inexpensive (around €12 per day for a 50cc machine, lower if you hire for three days or more). However, there are dangers in motor-scooter rental. Every year, there are a number of serious injuries and fatalities involving riders. The government has recently passed legislation making it illegal to rent a machine with any size engine without a bike license.

Many rental agencies have not passed on this information to hirers. If you rent a bike without a bike license, any insurance you have will be null and void, creating grave difficulties for you if you are injured or involved in an accident.

Those who rent bikes or mopeds should wear helmets. Although it is rarely enforced, it is the law in Greece. They should also proceed with caution, especially on corners where ground dust and gravel make the road surface slippery.

BUDGETING FOR YOUR TRIP

Once you have reached the Greek islands, living is relatively cheap. Food prices are controlled by the Greek government, and they rarely rise above the rate of inflation every year. Ferry travel and domestic flights are also affordable.

Here are some sample costs for goods and services in the islands:

Double room in moderately priced hotel	€50–75.
One-day car rental	€50–80.
One-day motor scooter rental	€12.
Three-course dinner for one, without drinks	€15–20.
One-way bus fare Parikia – Naoussa on Paros	€1.
Taxi from Skiathos Airport to town	€3.
Commercial ferry ticket for one passenger, Mykonos – Paros	€5.
Entrance fee to an archaeological site	€4.
Half-hour Jet-ski rental	€12.
Two-tank dive	€90.

CAMPING

The climate of the Greek islands makes them a popular place for camping. The GNTO has a booklet with information about authorized camp sites on various islands, or you may wish to contact the Hellenic Camping Association directly at 102 Solonos Street, 106 80, Athens; Tel/fax 362 1560.

CAR RENTAL/HIRE (see also DRIVING)

Most islands have cars for rental/hire, but think before you commit yourself. The primary roads on the major islands are usually in good condition, but if you want to explore secluded areas, the secondary roads may be of poor quality and require a 4-wheel-drive vehicle.

On smaller or more popular islands, the local bus service may be adequate, with frequent service running from early morning until 11pm or later. Although out of season, buses may not run at all during siesta (2pm–5pm) or after 6pm in the evening.

The following islands are large enough that vehicle rental would certainly enhance your stay and free you from complicated bus schedules: Tinos, Naxos, Paros, Skyros, Skopelos, Lesvos, Chios, Samos, and Kos.

Booking through a major international firm before you arrive will guarantee your vehicle, which can be useful, especially in peak season when demand is high. Hertz, Avis, and Alamo all service the islands, as does Europcar (Tel. 9622402) and Budget (Tel. 3426226).

However, there are many reputable local rental agencies, including Sixt Rent a Car and Reliable International. You may also find that local companies are more flexible with regard to price, especially in low season.

Most major car-rental firms companies have offices at the island airport. If not, there may be an extra charge to deliver your car to the airport or to your hotel. Always ask if services, such as delivery, cost extra as the total fee for your rental may be disproportionately high with delivery included.

Those who wish to rent should carry an International Driving Permit, although a national driving license is usually accepted (provided it has been held for one full year and the driver is over 21 years of age). Deposits are usually waived for those paying by credit card.

Insurance Insurance is often included in the rental rate, but inquire to be sure. The collision damage waiver is advisable. If your credit card or home insurance policy does not provide it, you should purchase it as part of your rental agreement.

 C

CLIMATE

The Greek islands have a short, warm but rainy spring, a long, hot summer, a warm autumn, and a cool winter. The northern islands are always a couple of degrees cooler than the southernmost. The islands are swept constantly by Meltemi winds, which blow from the Caucasus Mountains of Russia across the Black Sea and down into the Aegean. The Meltemi winds blow warm air in summer, but sometimes bitterly cold air in winter. The Cyclades are the most affected, where the winds can change daily.

Below is a chart of average monthly temperatures and rainfall for Naxos in the central Cyclades.

	J	F	M	A	M	J	J	A	S	O	N	D
max. C°	14	15	16	19	23	26	27	28	26	24	20	17
F°	57	59	61	67	73	78	81	82	78	75	68	62
min. C°	10	9	11	13	16	20	22	22	21	18	14	12
F°	50	49	51	56	61	68	72	72	69	64	58	53

CLOTHING

In summer, you'll require very little clothing in the Greek islands. In daytime, think about swimwear plus a light layer to protect you from sunburn, and sandals. For sightseeing, dress shorts or lightweight pants and T-shirts are appropriate for men and women. Women will also be comfortable in lightweight dresses. Natural fibers like cotton and silk are ideal, as they help to wick away perspiration and allow the skin underneath to breathe. Be sure to pack comfortable walking shoes for touring archaeological sites.

If you intend to visit churches or monasteries, appropriate dress is compulsory. Both sexes should cover their shoulders. Men should wear lightweight slacks and women should wear a skirt that covers the knees.

Don't forget a hat and good sunglasses. Whitewashed buildings reflect the sun, creating a lot of glare that can tire eyes very quickly.

In the evening, the islands are relaxed. Very few places have a dress code, although visitors like to change for the evening. A light sweater would be useful for chilly evenings, especially in early or late season. Both spring and autumn can be cool after the sun has dropped. It can also get remarkably chilly after dark on the decks of ferries, so if you take a day trip and intend to return late, a cotton sweater or fleece jacket might be welcome.

COMPLAINTS (see also EMERGENCIES)

If you have a complaint, it's best to raise it first with the proprietor of the establishment concerned. If you are not satisfied, then take your complaint to the tourist police (for telephone numbers, see EMERGENCIES). There is a contingent of officers on each island who deal solely with the security of visitors and process complaints of any kind. These officers speak English.

CRIME AND SAFETY (see also EMERGENCIES)

The Greek islands are relatively safe both in terms of your personal safety and the safety of your belongings. Most visitor problems tend to center around motor scooter accidents and overindulgence in sun or alcohol. Serious crime is rare; however it is still important to guard against becoming a victim. Islands with the highest visitor numbers have reported an increase in theft and other petty crime, so make sure that you take the following precautions: Lock any valuables in the hotel safe. Don't leave valuables unsupervised on the beach or in view in your rental car.

If you find yourself a victim of crime, contact the tourist police on the island concerned (for numbers on the main islands, see EMERGENCIES). These officers speak English.

CUSTOMS AND ENTRY REQUIREMENTS (see also
ANTIQUITIES)

Citizens of Great Britain and Ireland, as EU citizens, can visit the Greek islands for an unlimited amount of time, but British citizens must have a valid passport. Citizens of Ireland can enter with a valid identity card or passport. Citizens of the US, Canada, Australia, and New Zealand can stay for up to three months with a valid passport. South African citizens can stay for up to two months on a valid passport. No visas are needed for these stays. If you wish to extend these timeframes, you must obtain a permit from the Aliens Bureau, 173 Alexandras Avenue, 11 522, Athens; Tel. 770 5701.

Visitors may import and export up to €10,000. There are no restrictions on traveler's checks; however sums of over $1,000 or its equivalent must be declared on entry.

Greece has some strict regulations regarding the import of drugs. All the obvious ones are illegal and there are strict laws with strong punitive measures for anyone breaking the rules. Note that some seemingly benign drugs such as codeine or tranquilizers are also banned. If you take any drug on the advice of your doctor, always carry enough for your needs in an official container (medicines for personal use are permitted).

Since the abolishment of duty-free allowances for all EU countries (as of July 1999), all goods brought into Greece from Britain and Ireland must be duty paid. In theory, there are no limitations to the amount of duty-paid goods that can be brought into the country. However, be aware that cigarettes and most spirits are much cheaper in Greece than in Britain and Ireland (government duty is much lower in Greece), therefore waiting until you reach your destination to buy these goods will save you money.

For citizens of non-EU countries, allowances for goods bought duty-free to be carried into Greece or the islands are as follows: 200

cigarettes or 50 cigars or 250 grams of tobacco; 1 liter of spirits or 4 liters of wine; 250 ml of cologne or 50 ml of perfume.

 D

DRIVING

Road Conditions The roads in the Greek islands have improved greatly in the last few years, although there are still great differences between A roads and B roads. The latter usually require a 4-wheel-drive vehicle.

Most of the primary roads on the main islands have decent road surfaces, however the roads have no shoulders, only dust and stones at the side of the gravel. This can cause problems if you need to slow and leave the carriageway, especially for bike riders who need to drive toward the center of the paved surface, to avoid the loose surface. If you get caught in a summer storm, the road surface can become very slippery.

Many roads climb up steep inclines with no protection between the road and the drop beside the road. This requires a degree of concentration, especially where roads narrow and climb by switchback turns.

Rules and Regulations Greece drives on the right and passes on the left, usually yielding to vehicles from the right. Most road signs are international and easily understood, however one problem in navigating can be a lack of Roman transliterations of place names on road signs (just the Greek lettering appears).

The speed limit is 100 km/h (65 mph) on open roads; in towns, it is 50 km/h (30 mph), unless otherwise stated. Many drivers do not adhere to the regulations. Both speed limit and distance signs are in kilometers.

Seat belts are compulsory, as are crash helmets when riding a motor scooter, but both are rarely used. Drunk driving laws are strict. Road patrols are common, with Breathalyzer tests and on-the-spot fines.

Many island towns have one-way system streets. Be aware that many motor scooter riders (and some car drivers) do not obey these rules. Many scooter riders are inexperienced and may not be properly insured. Give them a wide berth.

Pedestrians also have their own agendas. They will often walk in the roadway, and step out without looking. In towns, you may find a large number of backpackers who, carrying large and heavy packs in the heat, find it difficult to move out of the way. They appreciate a little latitude on the part of drivers.

Fuel Costs Fuel is extremely cheap by European standards at around €0.80 per liter. When exploring a large island, it's wise to anticipate your fuel needs, as gas/petrol stations tend to be found only around the main towns. Gas stations are open every day in season between the hours of 9am and 7pm.

Parking Parking lots are marked by a sign with a white "P" on a blue background. There is generally one public parking area in every major town, usually near the port. Most of the islands have painted lines along the roadside indicating whether parking is allowed. If you decide to park along the road, always check to make sure you are not creating a hazard for other drivers and users of the road. Do not park at intersections or near junctions, and do not block entrances. Unless they are situated in old town centers, which tend to be for pedestrians only, most hotels and restaurants have parking.

If You Need Help The Greek National Touring Club (ELPA) at 2 – 4 Messogion Street, Athens; Tel. 779 1615, provides emergency road assistance (Tel. 104) in Greece, but in the islands this service is not comprehensive. Always take the local telephone number of your car-rental firm when picking up your car or arranging for its delivery to you. If necessary, they can organize aid for you.

Road Signs Most road signs are the standard pictographs used throughout Europe. However, you may also meet some of these written signs:

ΑΔΔΔΙΕΞΧΕΟΔΔΔΟΣΣΣ	No through road
ΑΛΛΛΤ/ΣΣΣΤΟΜ	Stop
ΑΝΩΩΩΜΑΛΛΛΙΑ ΟΔΔΔΟΣΣΣΤΡΩΩΩΜΑΤΟΣΣΣ	Bad road surface
ΑΠΠΠΑΓΓΓΟΡΕΥΕΤΑΙ Η ΕΙΣΣΣΟΔΔΔΟΣΣΣ	No entry
ΑΠΠΠΑΓΓΓΟΡΕΥΕΤΑΙ Η ΣΣΣΤΑΘΘΔΔΜΕΥΣΣΣΙΣΣΣ	No parking
ΔΔΔΙΑΒΑΣΣΣΙΣΣΣΠΡΠΕΖΩΩΩΝ	Pedestrian crossing
ΕΡΓΓΓΑ ΕΠΡΠΙ ΤΗΣΣΣ ΟΔΔΔΟΥ	Road work in progress
ΚΙΝΔΔΔΥΝΟΣΣΣ	Caution
ΜΟΝΟΔΔΓΓΡΟΜΟΣΣΣ	One-way traffic
ΠΠΠΑΡΑΚΑΜΠΠΠΤΗΡΙΟΣΣΣ	Diversion (detour)

Are we on the right road for…? **Ímaste stosostó drómo giá…?**

Full tank, please. **Na to gemísete me venzíni.**

normal/super/lead-free **aplí/soúper/amólivdos**

My car has broken down. **Épatha mía vlávi.**

There's been an accident. **Égine éna disteíchima.**

Fluid measures

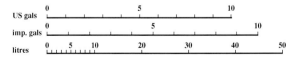

Distance

E

ELECTRICITY

The electric current in Greece and the islands is 220 volts/50 cycles. Electric plugs are of the European/continental two- or three-prong variety. Adapter plugs are available in the main islands from electrical stores, but it's better to bring your own.

EMBASSIES AND CONSULATES

Most countries have embassies and consulates in Athens, however some operate consular services on the islands.

Australia	37 D. Soutsou Street, 115-21, Athens; Tel. 645-0404; fax 646-6595
Canada	4 Gennadiou Street, 115-21, Athens; Tel. 727-3400; fax 727-3460
Ireland	7 Vass. Konstantinou Avenue, 106-74, Athens; Tel. 723-2771/2; fax 724-0217
New Zealand	24 Xanias Street, 115-28, Athens; Tel. 771- 0112; fax 777-7390
South Africa	60 Kifissias Avenue, 151-25, Maroussi; Tel. 680-6645; fax 680-6640
United Kingdom	1 Ploutarchou Street, 106-75, Athens; Tel. 723-6211; fax 724-1872 or 723-0954
US	91 Vass. Sophias Avenue, 115-27, Athens; Tel. 721-2951; fax 645-6282

The UK also has the following regional consulates in the islands:

Kos	Tel. (02420)-21549; fax (02420)-25948
Syros	Tel. (02810) 82232; fax (02810)-83293

EMERGENCIES

Police presence on the islands is limited, and patrol cars are almost non-existent, although the chance of needing their help is also minimal. To reach the police, dial 100. There are tourist police officers on duty. These officers are specially trained to deal with visitor problems and speak English.

Here are the telephone numbers for the major islands:

Mykonos	Tel. 23990
Santorini	Tel. 22649
Kos	Tel. 22222
Skiathos	Tel. 21111

For medical emergencies, dial 166.

G

GAY AND LESBIAN TRAVELERS
The island of Mykonos is one of the most gay-friendly destinations in Europe, with many beaches, hotels, bars, and clubs specifically catering to gay and lesbian travelers (although gay and lesbian travelers are by no means limited to these places). July and August are the best months to meet like-minded people from all over Europe and take part in the most manic nightlife.

GETTING THERE (see also AIRPORTS, DRIVING)

By Air International scheduled flights will almost always land at Eleftherinos Venizolos International Airport. For the northern Aegean Islands (Thassos, Limnos, and Samothraki), it may be possible to fly directly to Thessaloniki on the northern Greek mainland for ferry connections or onward flights.

The national airline for Greece and the Aegean Islands is Olympic Airways. It operates direct flights to and from the following destinations in the US: New York (JFK) daily and Boston twice a week. In the UK, London Gatwick and Heathrow airports have daily flights; Manchester Airport also has flights several times a week, as does Glasgow Airport. In Canada, there are flights to and from Montreal and Toronto twice a week. In Australia, Sydney has flights twice a week.

Greek Islands

Delta has direct flights from JFK Airport in New York.

Other major airlines that operate flights to Athens, which may form major hubs for travelers from the US, South Africa, Ireland, and Australasia are: British Airways through their hub in London, KLM with a hub in Amsterdam, Lufthansa which travels via Frankfurt, and Sabena (Belgian Airlines) through Brussels.

Many other national carriers can reach these European hubs to connect with flights to Athens, including Quantas, Air New Zealand, Thai Airlines (serving Australia and New Zealand via Bangkok), South African Airlines, and American Airlines.

From Athens, Olympic Airways operates daily flights to the following Greek Islands: Chios, Kastellorizo (daily in summer only), Kos, Limnos, Milos, Mykonos, Lesvos (Mytilini), Naxos, Paros, Samos, Santorini (Thira), Skiathos, and Syros, and operates several flights per week to Astypalea, Karpathos, and Skyros.

Olympic Airways will sometimes offer internal flights at a reduced rate for travelers who have flown into Greece on the airline. Ask about special deals before you make reservations. Unfortunately, it is almost impossible to travel from island to island by plane without returning to Athens, the hub of the system.

Direct charter flights from Britain also travel to Kos, Skiathos, Lesvos, and Mykonos during the summer months from London Gatwick, Manchester, and many regional airports.

By Sea Travel to Athens and then take a ferry to your chosen island from the main harbors of Piraeus or Rafina on the Greek mainland. Travel from Eleftherinos Venizolos International Airport to the port of Piraeus for onward ferry journeys can be undertaken by taxi or bus (see AIRPORTS above for details).

Cruising is a popular option, and a comfortable way to see several islands in a short space of time. A number of companies offer the Aegean Islands as an itinerary (Mykonos/Delos and Santorini are favorites), with starting ports of either Istanbul or Athens. Ships offer different levels of service, and thus price ranges, so research is imperative in order to get the package that suits your taste and budget. Cunard is one of the long-standing companies. Visit their web site <www.cunardline.com> for further information. Royal Olympic Cruise Line is a company based in Greece. You can find them on the Web at <www.royalolympiccruises.com>.

By Car The direct road route to Greece and the islands from Western Europe takes travelers through the former Yugoslavia, which for obvious reasons has been less popular in recent years. However, for those who want to travel from Western Europe with a vehicle, there are several ferry companies that operate services from ports in Italy to ports on the Greek mainland, thereby bypassing the trouble spot. Patras to Bari (17 hours) and Patras to Ancona (20 hours) are the main routes. Two operators are Superfast Ferries, 157 Alkyonidon Avenue, 166-73, Voula, Athens; Tel. (010) 969-1100, fax (010) 969-1190, web site <www.superfast.com>; and Strintzis Lines, 26 Akti Possidonis, 185-31, Piraeus; Tel. (010) 414-1230; fax (010) 422-5256, web site <www.strintzis.gr>.

In order to enter Greece, you must have the vehicle registration document, a nationality plate, and proof of insurance (a comprehensive plan is advised).

By Rail Traveling through Europe to Greece by train poses the same problems car travel does, because all major rail services travel through the war-torn states of what was once Yugoslavia. Rail travel can still be accomplished by taking services to the Italian ferry ports and taking a boat as per the "By Car" section above. Eurorail has several combination tickets, including special fares for those who are under age 26 and senior citizens. Further details can be obtained by accessing the company's web site at <www.eurorail.com>.

GUIDES AND TOURS

If you wish to contract the services of an English-speaking guide, contact the GNTO (EOT in the islands) to discuss possibilities on each island (see TOURIST INFORMATION). Taxi drivers will undertake half-day tours for an agreed fee, but will not act as guides.

Each island has travel agencies that can arrange itineraries and activities. Below are ones that we have found particularly helpful: Nirvana Tours on the seafront at Petra on Lesvos, Tel. (02530) 41991, fax (02530) 41992; Theokritos Travel on the main street in Tigaki on Kos; Tel. (02420) 69666, fax (02420) 69112.

H

HEALTH AND MEDICAL CARE (see also CUSTOMS AND ENTRY REQUIREMENTS)

In a medical emergency, dial 166. Each island has a hospital with doctors who speak reasonable English.

Emergency treatment is given free of charge to visitors, but this covers only immediate treatment. EU residents (UK and Irish nationals) will be able to get further free treatment, but must carry the form E111 to obtain it. E111 forms must be validated before you leave the UK. This is done at the post office before you leave for your trip.

It is always advisable to take out health/accident insurance to cover you for a health emergency while on vacation. Insurance will reimburse the cost of protracted treatment, an air taxi from smaller islands to the nearest major hospital, or repatriation should the need arise.

There are no vaccination requirements for the Greek islands.

The Greek islands do have scorpions and snakes, although not in great numbers, and they tend only to be found off the beaten track. When exploring archaeological sites, it is always wise to watch your footing and make some noise to ensure that the creatures have time to escape before you arrive. A more common nuisance is the mosquito, especially on a balmy night. Always carry and use anti-mosquito spray when walking in the undergrowth and when the sun sets.

Spiny sea urchins cause a number of injuries each year when people step on them while swimming. Avoidance is the best option, so invest in plastic sandals to protect your feet.

The sun is strong in Greece, especially as the summer breezes seem to cool the air, so it is important to use appropriate protection. Limit your time in the sun, apply sunblock regularly, and always carry a cover-up with you in case of overexposure. Children's skin should be always be well-protected when they are out in the sunshine.

Go easy on alcohol (it can cause dehydration). Tap water is safe to drink; however, bottled water often tastes better and is universally available. Always carry water with you to the beach or when sightseeing to protect against dehydration.

Pharmacies A pharmacy or *pharmakio* is marked by a sign with a green cross. Most pharmacists speak some English and will dispense medical advice for minor ailments (such as sunburn).

HOLIDAYS

During national holidays, government offices close along with most museums and archaeological sites. Restaurants and shops may remain open, especially during the tourist season. National holidays fall on the following dates:

1 January	New Year's Day or *Protochroniá*
6 January	Epiphany or *ton*
25 March	Greek Independence Day
1 May	May Day
15 August	Assumption of the Virgin
28 October	"No" Day
25 December	Christmas Day
26 December	St. Stephen's Day

Moveable dates occur around Easter. The first day of Lent (Clean Monday), Good Friday, Easter Monday, the Ascension, and Holy Monday (Whit Monday) change with every calendar year.

L

LANGUAGE

The Greek language of Homer and the ancients is no longer spoken in daily life. There are two Greek languages: *katharévousa*, which is the language of the elite, the courts, and of the ancient texts; and *dimotikí*, which is the language written and spoken by most Greeks today.

Most people working within the tourist industry have a basic English vocabulary and many speak English very well.

The table below lists the Greek letters in their capital and small forms, followed by the letters to which they correspond in English.

A	α	a	α	a as in bar
B	β	b	β	v
G	Γ	g	γ	g as in go*
D	Δ	d	δ	d like **th** in **th**is
E	ε	e	ε	e as in get
Z	ζ	z	ζ	z
H	ή	h	ή	i like **ee** in meet
Q	Θ	q	θ	th as in thin
I	ι	i	ι	like **ee** in meet
K	κ	k	κ	k
L	Λ	l	λ	l
M	μ	m	μ	m
N	ν	n	ν	n
X	Ξ	x	ξ	x like **ks** in thanks
O	o	o	o	as in go t
P	Π	p	π	p
P	ρ	r	ρ	r
S	Σ	s	σ, ς	s as in kiss

T	τ	t	τ	t
Y	υ	u	υ	i like **ee** in meet
F	Φ	j	φ	f
X	χ	c	χ	ch as in Scottish lo**ch**
Y	Ψ	y	ψ	ps as in ti**ps**y
O	Ο/Ω	w	ω	o as in got
OY	ου	ou	ου	oo as in soup

*except before **i-** and **e-**sounds, when it's pronounced like y in yes.

You'll find the *Berlitz Greek Phrase Book and Dictionary* covers nearly all the situations you're likely to encounter in your travels.

M

MAPS

Toubis prints maps that cover all of the Aegean Islands. The maps are simple but feature the main tourist sites and the road network (M. Toubis S.A.; Tel. 992-3874, web site <www.toubis.gr>). They are available at most bookstores and newsagents.

MEDIA

The only English-language newspaper that offers insight into Greek and world affairs is *Athens Today*, which can be bought at most major newsagents. There is at least one newsagent on each of the main islands, either near the port or at the town square. Major English-language newspapers can be bought on the most-visited islands, although they will be at least one day old. All United Kingdom dailies can be purchased, along with the *New York Times*.

If it is important to be totally up-to-date, then try getting online at one of the internet cafés that are springing up on islands such as Paros, Naxos, Mykonos, and Santorini.

Most hotels do not have satellite TV services. A few may offer an English-language TV news service — generally BBC News 24 — along with services in other languages.

Greek Islands

MONEY

Currency Greece's monetary unit is the *Euro* (abbreviated €), which is divided into 100 *cents*. Banknotes are available in denominations of 500, 200, 100, 50, 20, 10 and 5 Euros. There are coins for 2 and 1 Euro, and for 50, 20, 10, 5, 2 and 1 cent.

Currency Exchange Most banks offer currency exchange for foreign currencies and travelers' checks, charging a commission for the service that varies, but is usually between 1% and 3%. Exchange rates should be published on a notice board inside the bank or in the window, and are generally the same for each bank.

You can also exchange money and traveler's checks at commercial exchange shops found in the tourist centers of the main islands. These shops are often open longer hours than banks. Some of them advertise commission-free transactions, but exchange rates vary, so you'll need to judge which establishment offers the better deal.

You will always need to prove your identity when exchanging money, so take your passport with you.

Traveler's Checks These are best exchanged for cash at banks or exchange shops rather than being used to buy goods directly.

Automatic Teller Machines (ATMs) Using an ATM is the most convenient way of obtaining euros, and depending on your own individual card charges, it might also be the cheapest. There is a good network of ATMs throughout the major islands that will accept both major credit cards (MasterCard and Visa) and debit cards (Cirrus and Plus). However, long lines can develop when islands become busy, and machines can be either empty or out of order, so it would not be sensible to rely on ATMs as your sole means of obtaining cash.

Credit Cards Many hotels, restaurants, ticket offices, and shops accept credit cards, but there is still a sizeable minority which do not. Some may charge extra for credit card payments, to cover their extra costs. It is always advisable to ask about credit card acceptance before you sign the register or order your food, to avoid difficulties later. It may also help to carry cash — perhaps $25–$35 (£15–£25) per person per day — to cover meals, rather than rely on your credit card. On the more remote islands, cash is always the safest bet for everyday transactions.

OPENING HOURS

Opening hours can be a little complicated. They vary greatly between high and low season on the most popular islands. Always be aware that the siesta is an important part of the day, and most establishments will close in the afternoon because of it.

Banks are open Mon–Thurs 8am–2pm, Fri 8am–1:30pm.

Most museums are open Mon–Fri 8am–2pm and 5pm–7pm (this will vary). Most archaeological sites are closed on Monday.

Shops are open Mon–Sat 8am–2pm and 5pm–8:30pm, although in peak season, they may stay open until midnight. Post offices open Mon–Sat 8am–2pm; on larger islands, they may remain open until 7pm.

P

POLICE (see also Emergencies)
To reach the police, dial 100. To reach the tourist police on a particular island, consult the list below:

Kos	Tel. (02420) 22222
Mykonos	Tel. (02890) 23990
Santorini	Tel. (02860) 22649
Patmos	Tel. (02470) 31303
Skiathos	Tel. (04270) 21111

POST OFFICES

Post office signs are painted bright yellow with the initials ELTA. They are generally open from 8am–2pm. Stamps can be bought here at cost and from newsagents for a small premium. Parcels for non-EU countries should not be sealed until they have been checked by post office staff. Post offices also handle currency exchange, check cashing, and money orders. Postage for a postcard to the UK is around €0.70, and it generally takes five to seven days to arrive.

PUBLIC TRANSPORTATION

Most islands have a good bus service that connects all major settlements and beaches. A small central bus station posts a timetable for each route, with regular, generally on-time service. Buses may stop during the afternoon siesta, although this is generally the case only on small islands. Fares are low. In addition, a small boat (caique) service runs from major resorts to popular beaches. These boats are also cheap and reliable.

R

RELIGION

The Greek Orthodox religion is most prevalent throughout the islands. There are also Catholic churches on a few islands, notably Tinos and Naxos.

T

TELEPHONE

The country code for Greece is 30. To call overseas from the Greek islands, dial 00, then the country code, then the telephone number. For reference, Australia is 61, South Africa is 27, Canada is 1, the UK is 44, Ireland is 353, New Zealand is 64, and the US is 1.

There are many card operated telephone booths throughout the islands, usually at ports. Directions appear in English on most machines. Newsagents and hotels sell telephone cards which can be used for domestic and direct-dial international calls.

TIME ZONES

Greece is two hours ahead of Greenwich mean time (GMT). The chart below references it against other major time zones.

	New York	London	**Aegean**	Jo'burg	Sydney	Auckland
winter:	5am	10am	**12noon**	12noon	9pm	11pm
summer:	5am	10am	**12noon**	11am	7pm	9pm

TIPPING

Service is included in restaurant and bar bills, although it is customary to leave any small change on the table.

Taxi drivers expect a 10% tip. Hotel chambermaids should be left a tip of around €1 per day. Bellhops and doormen should be tipped up to €2 depending on services provided. Attendants in toilets should be left around €0.30.

TOILETS

You will generally find public toilets near the market squares in most major towns on the islands; look for the international signs of a figure of a man or a woman. They are of varying degrees of cleanliness and will often be of a "hole in the floor" design rather than a sit-down pan.

Most cafés and bars have clean facilities, although these may be basic. It is customary to buy a drink at an establishment if you wish to use the toilets. On beaches, the bars and cafés have toilets. Remember, never put toilet tissue into the toilet; Greek drains become clogged very easily. Always use the receptacle provided. If there is an attendant present, it is customary to leave a small tip.

TOURIST INFORMATION

The Greek National Tourist Organization (GNTO) or Ellinikos Organismos Tourismu (EOT) is responsible for producing and dispersing tourist information. They have a network of offices throughout the world, but official representation in the islands is very scant. This leaves the market open to lots of unofficial information bureaus, which vary greatly in quality. For tourist information before you travel to Greece, contact one of the following offices:

Australia and New Zealand	51-75 Pitt Street, Sydney, New South Wales (P.O. Box R203, Royal Exchange, New South Wales, 2000, Australia); Tel. (2) 92411663-5; fax 92352174
Canada	1300 Bay Street, Main Level, Toronto, Ontario M5R 3K8, Canada; Tel. (416) 968-2220; fax (416) 968-6533; e-mail <gnto.tor@sympatico.ca>
	1170 Place du Frère André, Suite 300, Montreal, Quebec H3B 3C6, Canada; Tel. (514) 871-1535; fax (514) 871-1498
UK and Ireland	4 Conduit Street, London W1R 0DJ, UK; Tel. (020) 7734 5997; fax (020) 7287 1369; e-mail <eot-greektouristoffice@btinternet.com>
US	Olympic Tower, 645 Fifth Avenue, New York, NY 10022; Tel. (212) 421-5777; fax (212) 826-6940; e-mail <gnto@greektourism.com>

For tourist information in the Aegean, official GNTO/EOT offices can be found at the following addresses:

Athens	2 Amerikis Street, P.O. Box 1017, 105-64 Athens; Tel. (010) 327-1300; fax (010) 322-4184
Cyclades Islands	10 Dodecanissou Street, 841-00, Syros; Tel. (08210) 86725; fax (08210) 82375
Limnos	Provincial Buildings of Limnos, 814-00, Limnos; Tel. (02540) 22996
Northeast Aegean	6 T. Aristarchou Street, 811-00, Mytilini (Lesvos), Tel. (02510) 42511; Airport at Mytilini (Lesvos), Tel. (02510) 61279
Samos	4 25th March Street, 831-00, Samos; Tel. (02730) 28530

W

WEB SITES

There are a number of web sites to help you plan your trip. Although information and sites are changing constantly, here are some that should prove useful: <www.greecetravel.com>, <www.helios.gr>, <www.grecian.net>, and <www.gtpnet.com>.

WEIGHTS AND MEASURES

Length

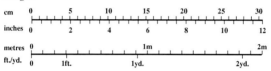

Weight

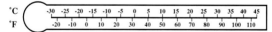

Temperature

Y

YOUTH HOSTELS

The Greek Youth Hostel Association (4 Dragatsaniou Street, 105-59, Athens, Tel. 323-4107) can provide information about hosteling in the islands. We can recommend two youth hostels in Santorini (Kamares Youth Hostel, Erythrou Stavrou, Tel. (02860) 22387; and Kondohori Youth Hostel, Agios Eleftherios, Tel. (02860) 22722), but the many cheap private rooms around the islands make the need for hostels less pressing than elsewhere.

Recommended Hotels

Although there is a great deal of accommodation scattered throughout the Aegean Islands, the majority of it is in the lower quality range, with many C-rated hotels and unclassified small studio apartments. If you intend to travel in the summer months and want a good quality hotel, always make a firm reservation before you travel. If you arrive without a booking, there are a number of private agencies that advertise booking services. You will generally find them at the port.

Prices vary greatly during the short season with the highest rates from early July to the end of August. In early season (Easter–mid-June) and late season (after mid-September), deals are possible.

Most hotels will make a booking for room only or bed and breakfast. You can book American plan (in Europe, this is full board), but for most people, eating out is one of the best parts of an Aegean Island vacation.

As a guide to room prices, we have used the following euro symbols for double occupancy with bath, including breakfast, mid-season:

€€€€€	over 75 euros
€€€€	60–75 euros
€€€	45–60 euros
€€	30–45 euros
€	under 30 euros

THE CYCLADES

Mykonos

Belvedere Hotel €€€€ *Rochari, 84600, Mykonos; Tel. 2890-25122/5; fax (02890) 25126; web site: www.belvederehotel.com* Set just outside the hustle and bustle of the center of town, the Belvedere is housed in a white Cyclades-style building with an excellent pool. Internet facilities are provided, and Jacuzzi and steam baths are available. Guest laundry facilities. American-style buffet breakfast served daily 7–10:30am. Open year-round. 40 rooms. Major credit cards.

Leto Hotel €€€€ *Hora, 84600, Mykonos; Tel. (02890) 22207; fax (02890) 23985; e-mail <leto@leto.myk.forthnet.gr>.* An easy five-minute walk from the port, this property is ideally located. It's near the town museum (approximately ten minutes by foot from the town center) with excellent views across a small fishing harbor. Set in lush gardens with an attractive secluded pool. American-style buffet breakfast served daily 7–10:30am. Open year-round. 25 rooms. Major credit cards.

Tharroe of Mykonos €€€€€ *Hora, 84600, Mykonos; Tel. (02890) 27370/4; fax (02890) 27375.* Located just outside town, this luxury resort is housed in a typical Cyclades-style whitewashed building. All rooms have mini-bars, safes and telephones. 24-hour room service, fitness room, sauna, pool, and deck. Free transfers available. American-style buffet breakfast served daily 7–10:30am. Open year-round. 25 rooms. Major credit cards.

Theoxenia Hotel €€€ *Hora, 84600, Mykonos; Tel. (02890) 22230/23008; fax (02890) 22240; e-mail <theoxenia@leto.myk.forthnet.gr>.* Situated on the beach a little way south of Mykonos Town and near the windmills, the Theoxenia is housed in a traditional whitewashed building. Most rooms have a sea view. American-style buffet breakfast served daily 7–10:30am. Open April–October. 57 rooms. Major credit cards.

Tinos

Hotel Tinion €€ *1 Constantinou Alavanou, 84200, Tinos; Tel. (02830) 22261/24754; fax (02830) 24754.* A traditional, family-run hotel with simply furnished rooms. Located one street back from the harbor of Tinos Town. Some rooms with air-conditioning and balconies overlooking the street and harbor. Breakfast served daily 7–10am. Open April–October. 20 rooms. Major credit cards.

Paros

Astir of Paros €€€€€ *Kolymbithres, Naoussa, 84401, Paros; Tel. (02840) 51976; fax (02840) 51985; e-mail <astir@prometheus.hol.gr>.* An opulent resort hotel with a private beach, beautiful gardens, tennis courts, Jacuzzi, gym, and 3-hole golf course. All rooms have air-conditioning, telephones, mini-bars, TVs, and room service. Open April–November. 46 rooms. Major credit cards.

Lefkes Village Hotel €€€€€ *Lefkes, 84400, Paros; Tel. (02840) 41827; fax (02840) 41827. Winter: 137 Irakliou Avenue, 111 42, Athens; Tel. (01) 251 6497; fax (01) 253 3598.* This Cycladic-style hotel situated just outside Lefkes village has beautifully styled rooms and communal areas, a pool, and a terrace with majestic panoramic views down a verdant valley. The complex has a large garden, winery, and folklore museum. All rooms have air-conditioning, telephones, and mini-bars. Open April–end of October. 20 rooms of two, three, and four beds. Major credit cards.

Naxos

Hotel Grotta €€ *Hora (Naxos Town), 84300, Naxos; Tel. (02850) 22215; fax (02850) 22000; e-mail <grotta@naxos-island.com>.* A friendly, family-run hotel that's ideally situated on a hillside in the heart of the old town, within easy walking distance of the ferry port. Open April–October. 40 rooms. Cash only.

Mathiassos Village €€-€€€ *Hora, 84300, Naxos; Tel. (02850) 23300; winter Tel. (010) 291 8749 or (02850) 22318.* Bungalows built in the Cycladic style surrounded by large and verdant gardens on the outskirts of Hora. Facilities include a restaurant/café, swimming pool, children's playground, tennis court, and bus service to the beach (a ten-minute walk away). Open March–October. 110 rooms. Major credit cards.

Santorini

Fanari Traditional Cave Apartments €€€€€ *Oia, 84702, Santorini; Tel. (02860) 71008; fax (02860) 71235.* These refurbished, traditional cave houses have spectacular views (they spill down the caldera edge at the northern tip of Ia settlement, a five-minute walk from the town center). The pool is cut into a hillside, with half of it in the sunlight. Open April–October. 12 units. Major credit cards.

Hotel Veggara €€€€ *On the seafront, Perissa, 84700, Santorini; Tel. (02860) 82060; fax (02860) 82608; Athens office: 72 Archelaou Street, 13671, Thrakomakedones, Athens; Tel. (010) 243 1411; fax (010) 243 0168.* Housed in a neo-classical main building with surrounding Cycladic-style studios, the Veggara has pretty, well-appointed rooms. Two pools with a bar sit just off the beach. Studios and apartments have fully fitted kitchens. All accommodations have air-conditioning, TVs, telephones, and patios or balconies. Open May–November. 23 rooms, 9 studios, and 8 apartments. Major credit cards.

Santorini Palace €€€€ *Fira, 84700, Santorini; Tel. (02860) 22771; fax (02680) 23705; e-mail <spalace@otenet.gr>.* Situated a ten-minute walk from the center of Fira, the Santorini Palace sits 100 m (300 ft) from the caldera edge, with views over the coastal plains. The hotel has a pool with bar, a restaurant, and room service. Rooms have air-conditioning, telephones, satellite TVs, mini-bars, and hairdryers. Open year-round. 106 rooms. Major credit cards.

THE DODECANESE
Kos

Neptune Hotel €€€€ *Mastichari, 85300, Kos; Tel. (02420) 41480; fax (02420) 41574.* Perhaps the largest resort in the Aegean. Set among 170 acres in three separate developments, the Neptune is thirty minutes by car from Kos Town. Facilities include a sauna and Jacuzzi, tennis courts, three pools, three children's pools, a hairdresser, and a social program. All rooms have TVs, mini-bars, kitchenettes, safes, and hair dryers. Open April–November. 485 rooms. Major credit cards.

Paradise Hotel €-€€ *22 Odos Bouboulinas, Kos Town; Tel. (02420) 22988; fax (02420) 24205.* Located in the heart of Kos Town, this hotel is well situated for exploring nearby archaeo-logical sites, taking the ferry, or enjoying the nightlife. Basic rooms but extremely friendly service. Open May–October. 100 rooms. Major credit cards.

Patmos

Blue Bay Hotel €€€ *Skala, 85500, Patmos; Tel. (02470) 31165; fax (02470) 32303.* Situated a two-minute walk south of the town of Skala, the Blue Bay looks out over the entrance to the harbor. A small hotel, it has a no-smoking policy. Rooms are large and bright. There is also a bar and Internet café. Open April–October. 27 rooms. Cash only.

The Kastelli Hotel €€ *Skala, 85500, Patmos; Tel. (02470) 31361; fax (02470) 31656.* Set back from the seafront, this hotel stands behind the Skala Hotel. The rooms are clean and bright with balconies overlooking the harbor. Wonderful morning sunshine for early risers. Open year-round. 45 rooms. Cash only.

Skala Hotel €€€€ *Skala, 85500, Patmos; Tel. (02470) 31343; fax (02470) 31347; winter Tel. (010) 453 4000; fax (010) 453 0550; e-mail <skalahtl@12net.gr>.* Situated on the harborfront, the Skala is ideally located for exploring the village. It's close to the ferry, tavernas, and shopping. The hotel has a small pool and terrace, a bar and restaurant. All rooms have mini-bars. Open 1 April–31 October. 70 rooms. Major credit cards.

THE EASTERN AEGEAN

Lesvos

The Delfinia €€€ *Molyvos, 81108, Lesvos; Tel. (0253) 71373; fax (02530) 71524.* On the seafront at Molyvos, this hotel features rooms and bungalows. There's a good-size pool and beautiful views of the town. Rooms have telephones and balconies; bungalows have air-conditioning and mini-bars. Open year-round. 125 rooms. Major credit cards.

The Olive Press Hotel €€€€ *Molyvos, 81108, Lesvos; Tel. (02530) 71205; fax (02530) 71647.* This hotel was once an olive press and lies on the seafront where boats used to take barrels of oil away. A relaxing ambience pervades the whole establishment. Open April–October. 50 rooms. Major credit cards.

Hotel Sea Horse €€ *The Harbor, Molyvos, 81108, Lesvos; Tel. (02530) 71630; fax (02530) 71374.* Basic rooms with refrigerators, but all overlook the picturesque harbor. Open from Greek Easter to the end of October. 17 rooms. Cash only.

Hotel Votsala €€ *Thermi, GR, 81100, Lesvos; Tel. (02510) 71231; fax (02510) 71179; Winter: 17 Kydonion, Smyrni, GR, 17121, Athens; Tel/fax (01) 933 8887.* Set in a small spa village on the east coast of Lesvos, this small seashore hotel operates in a relaxed, house-party style. The owner leads archaeological walks for guests every week in summer. Restaurant and bar. All rooms have refrigerators and balconies. Open April–October. 42 rooms. Major credit cards.

Chios

Hotel Chios Chandris €€€ *Prokimea, Chios Town; Tel. (02710) 44401; fax (02710) 25768.* By Greek island standards, this is a high-rise hotel that dominates the harborfront. Rooms were updated in the late 1990s. Roof garden restaurant, large pool. Rooms have air-conditioning, mini-bars, and TVs. Open year-round. 156 rooms. Major credit cards.

Volissos Traditional Houses €€-€€€€ *Volissos Village, Chios; Tel. (02740) 21421; fax (02740) 21521.* Accommodation is in restored stone houses in a typical Greek village. All are tastefully and sympathetically decorated and sit among real family homes. Open April–October. 15 units of one or two bedrooms. Cash only.

Samos

Doryssa Bay Hotel and Village €€€€ *Pythagorio, 83100, Samos; Tel. (02730) 61360; fax (02730) 61463.* A large, modern resort complex with a swimming pool, tennis courts, water sports facility, and children's playground. Open April – October. 302 rooms. Major credit cards.

The Samos Hotel €€€-€€€€ *11 Themofolis Sofouli Street, 83100, Samos; Tel. (02730) 28377; fax (02730) 28482.* The Samos is on the promenade at Samos Town, near the ferry — a great location for touring the island. Facilities include swimming pool, Jacuzzi and 24 hour room service. Rooms contain TV, phone and balcony. Open all year. 50 rooms. Major credit cards.

THE SPORADES

Skiathos

Hotel Alkyon €€€ *Amoundia, Skiathos Town; Tel. (04270) 22981; fax (04270) 21643*. On the seafront just outside Skiathos Town, the Alkyon is close to restaurants and nightlife; the ferry is only a five-minute walk away. There's also a small pool. Open April–October. 88 rooms. Major credit cards.

Atrium Hotel €€€€ *37002, Skiathos; Tel. (04270) 49345; fax (04270) 49444*. Situated on a headland above pretty beaches, the Atrium is about fifteen minutes from Skiathos Town by bus. A beautifully styled hotel — the communal areas were based on traditional monastery buildings — there is a fitness room and large pool with terrace and bar. All rooms have patios or balconies, air-conditioning, and telephones. Open April–November. 75 rooms. Major credit cards.

Skiathos Palace €€€€€ *Koukounaries Beach, 37002, Skiathos; Tel. (04270) 22242; fax (04270) 49666*. A luxury resort set on the hillside above Koukounaries Beach. Facilities include a nightclub, swimming pool, sauna, water sports center, and tennis courts. Room service. Open May–October. 223 rooms. Major credit cards.

Skopelos

Skopelos Village €€€-€€€€ *Skopelos Town, 37003, Skopelos; Tel. (04240) 22517; fax (04240) 22958*. Ten minutes from Skopelos Town, this complex has a swimming pool, children's playground, and room service. Each apartment has a small kitchen and up to two bedrooms. Bus transfer to nearby beaches. Open April–October. 36 apartments. Major credit cards.

Recommended Restaurants

The following recommendations are scattered throughout the main Greek islands and range from authentic ouzeries and good value tavernas to some of the most renowned restaurants in the region. Some are a little difficult to find, having no address in the accepted sense. If this is the case, ask at your hotel for directions. A little effort to find authentic cuisine always pays dividends, so always be on the lookout for small back-street establishments that are sure to be frequented by local people.

Most restaurants do not operate on a booking system. Where reservations are recommended, we have indicated it in the description. The price categories used in this section are based on the cost of an entrée for one person. Prices for appetizers are very similar wherever you eat in the Aegean (Greek salads are around €3 and mezedes range from €2.50 to €5)

€€€€€	over 18 euros
€€€€	12–18 euros
€€€	8–12 euros
€€	4–8 euros
€	under 4 euros

THE CYCLADES

Mykonos

Edem €€€-€€€€ *near Panagia Panahrandou (the church at the top of the hill); Tel. (02890) 22855/23355.* Open year-round, daily 12 noon–1am. Upmarket restaurant set around a swimming pool. Very atmospheric in the evening, or you can have a swim before lunch! Greek dishes with a continental twist. Reservations recommended in peak season. Major credit cards.

Remvi €€€-€€€€ *at the Belvedere Hotel; Tel. (02890) 25122.* Open April–October, daily 8am–midnight. A relaxing and upmarket eatery with outstanding views over Mykonos Town from its terrace. Serves *à la carte* menu of Greek and Continental dishes that changes regularly. Reservations recommended. Major credit cards.

Taverna Antonini €€ *Platia Manto (where the taxi rank is); Tel. (02890) 22319.* Busy taverna spilling out onto a side street off the Platia Manto. Good Greek fare and friendly service since the 1950s. Cash only.

Taverna Vaggelis €€ *Platia Anomeras (the square in Ano Mera); Tel. (02890) 71577.* Open April–end of October, daily 11am–midnight. Typical Greek taverna with fresh fish and an open barbecue. Excellent dishes (staples of Greek cuisine) and a friendly atmosphere — a favorite with Greek families. Cash only.

Paros

Apollon €€€ *Market Street, 88400, Paros; Tel. (02840) 21875.* Open April–October, daily 5pm-midnight. Set in the buildings and walled gardens of an old olive press, the Apollon offers a relaxing ambience and wonderfully cooked Greek dishes. The food and service are worth the higher prices charged here. Major credit cards.

Babis Sarris € *Market Street, Parikia; Tel. (02840) 22702.* Open April–October, daily 9am-1am; November–May, Friday, Saturday, and Sunday only 9am-1am. Don't be put off by the modern décor of this psistaria, the salad ingredients and meat come from the family farm and add an extra delicious touch to the gyros, souvlakis, and Greek salads. Cash only.

Barbarossa €-€€€ *on the harbor at Naoussa, No phone.* Open year-round, daily 11am-11pm. This is only one of several authentic ouzeries along the harbor — all are good. Delicious mezedes are a specialty, especially octopus dishes. Sit with the old fishermen and watch the world go by. Cash only.

Naxos

Kastro €€ *Plateia Prandounas, Naxos Town; Tel. (02850) 22005.* Open year-round, daily 7pm–2am. Set in a small square with fine views over the harbor, the Kastro overflows with tables in summer and specializes in dishes made with locally caught rabbit. Try the rabbit stew with onions and red wine sauce. Cash only.

Santorini

Restaurant 1800 €€€€ *Odos Nikolaos Nomikos, Ia; Tel. (02860) 71485.* Open April–October daily for lunch 12 noon–4pm and dinner 7:30pm–1am. Set in a refurbished mansion (named after the date when it was originally built) which once belonged to a sea captain, this is one of the prettiest places on the island to eat or have a drink at the bar. Greek/continental dishes. Major credit cards.

Selene €€€-€€€€ *near the Artessena Hotel, Fira, Santorini; Tel. (02860) 23427.* Open year-round daily for lunch 12 noon–3pm and dinner 7pm–midnight. A superb setting on the caldera and fine cuisine with attention to detail has made Selene one of the premier restaurants in the Aegean. Greek dishes with an international accent. Reservations recommended. Major credit cards.

Taverna Nikolas €-€€€ *off the main square, Fira; Tel. (02860) 24550.* Open March–October, daily 12 noon–midnight. This small, family-run taverna is the place to meet local people. The food is freshly cooked daily, so there's no set menu. The dining room is always lively, and very busy — expect to line up. Cash only.

Vanilia €€€ *84700 Firostefani Square, Firostefani; Tel. (02860) 25931.* Open April–September daily for lunch 12 noon–4pm and dinner 5:30pm–1am. Situated on the crater, a ten-minute walk north of the center of Fira, this intimate restaurant offers a relaxing ambience. Whitewashed stone benches are covered with comfortable ethnic cushions and low lighting sets the scene. Several small rooms mean a quiet intimate dining experience. Greek and European dishes. Major credit cards.

THE DODECANESE

Kos

Petrino €€€-€€€€ *Plateia Theologou; Tel. (02420) 27251.* Open daily 5pm–midnight (closed mid-November–mid-December). The restaurant takes its name from the fact that it is housed in a traditional *petrino,* or residence. It is said to be the finest on the island, and the food and the setting are both exquisite and refined. The menu boasts several European dishes but also cooks its Greek dishes to perfection. The wine cellar is filled with the best domestic varieties. Major credit cards.

Taverna Ambeli €€-€€€ *Zipari, Kos; Tel. (02420) 69682.* Open April–October daily 10am–midnight, November–March daily 6pm–midnight. Family-run taverna lying to the west of Tigaki that serves delicious freshly cooked dishes and particularly good mezedes. Only the freshest ingredients are used here. Wonderful, home-produced country wine (from vines surrounding the dining terrace and blanketing nearby fields) is served from the barrel. In winter, log fires heat the interior dining room. Cash only.

Taverna Ampravis €€-€€€ *Ampravis hamlet, 1 km (1/2 mile) south of Kos Town; Tel. (02420) 25696.* Open April–October, daily 5pm–2am. With tables set in a verdant courtyard, this family-run restaurant offers some respite from the hubbub of Kos Town. Delicious Greek dishes, especially the dolmades, which is made in the traditional Dodecanese way with cabbage leaves. Cash only.

Patmos

Pantelis Restaurant €-€€ *on the street parallel to the seafront, Skala; Tel. (02470) 31230.* Open May–October, daily 11am–11pm. All the Greek staples in ample portions, which assures a good local clientele along with visitors waiting to catch ferries. Tables in the street or in the spacious dining room. Cash only.

Patmian House €€€-€€€€ *off Plateia Xanthos, Hora, Patmos; Tel. (02470) 31180.* Open Easter–October, daily 7pm–midnight. The reputation of this restaurant has spread across Greece and beyond. The setting in a restored 17th-century house has been featured in numerous architectural and travel magazines, and the food matches the surroundings. Greek/Continental dishes. Cash only.

Vagelis €€€ *Main Square, Chora; Tel. (02470) 31967.* Open May–October, daily noon–1am. Popular taverna with tables in the square or on a roof terrace. Greek dishes served with care by the long-standing owners. A good choice for a leisurely lunch after sightseeing, or a relaxing dinner. Major credit cards.

THE EASTERN AEGEAN

Lesvos

The Galley Restaurant €€-€€€ *The Harbor, Molyvos, No phone.* Open mid-April–late October, daily 12 noon–midnight. An English-run restaurant that uses the freshest local ingredients in an innovative way. Cash only.

O Rigas €€ *next to the Theophilos Hotel, Petra; Tel. (02530) 41405.* Open year-round, daily from 7pm. A typical, traditional taverna serving only a few freshly cooked dishes. Guests go into the kitchen to peruse the offerings before making their choice. No set menu but 100% authentic experience and delicious food. Cash only.

Chios

O Morias €€-€€€ *in the town square at Mesta, No phone.* Open year-round, daily for lunch 11am–3pm and dinner 6pm–midnight. Typical Greek taverna set in the heart of a medieval mastic village. Enjoy a leisurely lunch or hearty evening meal of traditional dishes. Cash only.

THE SPORADES
Skiathos

Taverna Asprolithos €€€-€€€€ *Odos Korai, Skiathos Town; Tel. (04270) 23110.* Open year-round, daily 7pm–1am. An elegant restaurant where service is more attentive than expected. The menu is mostly Greek, though prepared with a lighter hand and greater care, which is reflected in the price. Major credit cards.

Taverna Giorgios €€ *Trion Ierarchion Square (above the harbor), Skiathos Town. No phone.* Open April–October, daily 5pm–midnight. Set under a canvas on the cobbled street above the fishing harbor, this restaurant features barbecue meats that are cooked before your eyes. Choose whatever you think looks most appealing. Cash only.

Skopelos

Finikas Taverna €€-€€€ *at the top of Skopelos Town; Tel. (04240) 23247.* Open year-round, daily 6pm-midnight. Although difficult to find, this taverna is a relaxing place to eat, with views from its garden over the rooftops of Skopelos Town. Finikas often serves traditional dishes not found at most tavernas. Cash only.

INDEX

Agia Anna 31, 45
Agios Prokopios 45
Agnondas 76
Akrotiri 14, 46, 48, 50, 52
Alefkandra Quarter 30
Alonissos 8, 76-77
Anavatos 67-68
Andros 16, 27, 35-36, 38
Ano Mera 30
Antiparos 19-20, 39, 42
Apollon 44
Apollonia 39
Argenti Museum and Korai
    Library 66
Arsinoion rotunda 74
Artemon 39
Asclepium 52, 54
Asfendiou 55
Athenian empire 17
Athinios 46

Banana Beach 75, 79
Batsi 36
Bourdzi islet 75
Byzantine Empire 18, 24

Casa Romana 54
Castle of the Knights of St.
    John 52-53
Cave of St. Anne 56
Chalki 44
Chios 8, 15, 20-21, 24-25, 52,
    61, 64, 66-67, 70, 92, 95
Chora 19, 35, 45, 50, 56, 73, 90
Christianity 7, 18, 40, 73
Church of 100 Doors 38, 40
Church of Christ 76-77

Convent of the Apocalypse 52,
    56
Crusades 18, 24
Cycladic culture 13

Delos 7, 15-17, 27-35, 43, 52
Diafani 61
Dyo Chorio 38

Elia 31
Emborio 67
Ephesus 70
Exobourgo 38

Faltaïts Museum 78
Filoti 44
Fira 46-48, 50, 83, 90-91
Frankish castle 69

Gate of Parmenon 71
Gavrion 35-36
Golden Beach 41
Greek independence 20, 92
Grikos Bay 58

Hippocrates Tree 51, 53
Hora 43-44
Horio 60
House of Cleopatra 34
House of Dionysos 34
House of Dolphins 34
House of Masks 34
House of the Trident 34
Hrysopighi Monastery 39

Ia 47
Ios 25, 50-51, 79, 90

Kalymnos 27, 58-59, 88, 92
Kamares 39
Kamari 50, 54
Kambos 58, 66
Kardamena 54
Karpathos 60, 83, 88, 91-92
Kastro 39-40, 71, 73
Kavala 70
Kefalos 55
Keramoti 44
Kokari 69
Kokkinokastro Peninsula 78
Kolymbithres 40
Korinada 44
Koronos 44
Kos 8, 14, 19, 22, 27, 31, 51-
   55, 57, 80, 82, 90-92
Koukounaries Beach 72, 75
Krassi Beach 75
Krissi Amoudia 71
Kusadasi 70

Lalaria Beach 76
Lampis Bay 58
Lefkes 41, 83
Lesvos 8, 15, 20-21, 25, 52,
   59-65, 70, 88, 92, 95
Limin 70-71
Limnos 8, 25, 70-71, 92
Loggia Mosque 51, 53

Magazia Beach 78
Makriamos 71, 79
Mandamadhos 64
Marathi 41
Marathokambos 70
Massouri 60
mastihohoria 66
medieval castle 63

medieval kastro 66
Megaron Gyzi Museum 47
Mesta 67
Milopotamos 50, 79
Minoans 14
Mirties 60
Modern Art Museum 36
Molyvos 64-65
Monastery of Profitis Ilias 48
Monastery of St. John the
   Theologian 31, 52, 54, 56
Monastery of Taxiarhis 64
Monastery of
   Zoodohou Pighi 36
Moria 64
Moudros 72
Mount Fengari 73-74, 83
Mount Kerkis 70
Mount Kynthos 35
Mount Zas 44, 84
Myceneans 14
Mykonos 7, 12, 26-31, 33, 35,
   38, 52, 79, 81, 86-88, 90
Myrina 72-73
Mytilini 52, 59, 63-64, 91

Naoussa 40, 82
Naxos 15-16, 19, 27, 43-45,
   49, 80, 84, 88, 99
Nea Kameni 45
Nea Moni 52, 64, 67-68

Olimbos 61, 65, 83, 91
Ormos Ermou 63
Ottoman Empire 21, 51

Palea Kameni 45, 50
Panagia Ekatontapiliani 40
Panagia Evangelistria 37

Panagia Theoskepastos 43
Panormos 38, 76
Paradise Beach 12, 30, 81
Paraportiani Church 29
Parikia 40, 42
Paros 13, 15-16, 27, 35, 39-40,
    42, 79-81, 83, 91-92
Patitiri 77
Patmos 8, 18, 24, 31, 52, 55, 58
Perissa 47, 50, 81
Persian wars 16
Petaloudes 42
Petra 65
Petrified Forest 52, 62, 65
Petros 29
Pigadia 61
Pirgos 48
Piso Livadi 41
Pithagorio 67, 69
Platis Gialos 31, 39
Pothia 59-60
Psarou 31
Pyli 55
Pyrgi 67
Pyrgos 38, 88

Rhenia 30, 35
Roman Odeon 54

Sacred Lake 32-33
Sacred Way 32
Samos 8, 15, 20-22, 25, 61,
    67-70, 80
Samothraki 8, 25, 73-74, 83
Sanctuary of Apollo 33
Sanctuary of the Great Gods 73
Santorini 7-8, 14, 24, 31, 44-
    48, 50, 52, 79-81, 83, 86-
    87, 90-91

shrine to St. John the Baptist at
    Vrykounda 61
Sifnos 39, 88, 98
Skala Potamias 71
Skiathos 8, 27, 72, 75, 78-79,
    82, 90
Skopelos 8, 27, 74, 76-77
Skyros 8, 27, 78, 92
Sporades Marine Park 77
Stafylos Beach 76

Tarabados 38
Telendos 60
Temenos 74
Temple of Apollo 42-43
Temple of Hera 69, 71
Terrace of the Lions 33
Thasos 8, 25, 70-71, 74, 79,
    88, 90, 92
Theater Quarter 34-35
Theologos 71
Therma 74
Thira 8, 14, 45, 48
Thirasia 45, 50
Tigaki 54, 82
Tinos 20, 22, 27, 36-38, 83,
    88, 92
Tourliani Monastery 30
Tragea Valley 44, 84
Tris Boukes 78
Tunnel of Eupalinos 69

Vathi 39, 60, 68-69
Venetian kastro 42, 78
Volissos 68

Winged Victory of Samothraki
    74